Imminent Cosmic Event

This event will affect every person on this planet. It only happens once every 13,000 years. This document also includes Secret Government Projects that affect your life and that you need to know to survive, plus Proof of UFOs, Lessons from Quantum Physics, metaphysical concepts that Affect Your Life, and proven government conspiracies backed by government insiders.

by

Jason McCormick

ISBNs:

eBook: *978-1-966647-92-8*

Paperback: *978-1-966647-93-5*

Hardback: *978-1-966647-94-2*

Published by:

Authors Publishing House

178 Broadway, 3rd Floor, #1343

New York, NY 10001, USA

Main Line: *(855) 624-0155*

Email: *support@authorspublishinghouse.com*

Table of Contents

Preface

You're probably asking yourself, **"Why do I need the information in this book?"** You will gain a great deal of wisdom and more control over your life, and you will also become more knowledgeable than over 80% of the people about how our government influences your thoughts. They don't want you to be a critical thinker; instead, they desperately want you to be a sheep.

The information in my book will gradually enable you to eliminate the mind-control tactics that our government uses to program your mind to buy into their lies. Your mind is the most powerful asset that you have. You should not let anyone try to control it. Yet, the majority of people are clueless that their minds are being controlled. Most people do not understand that there is an evil element in our government, and I have the proof.

And know that this imminent cosmic event will change everyone's life on this planet. This planetary event has never been experienced before in the millions of years that our Mother Earth has existed. I've been told it will be approximately another 35 years before this happens. Some of us will not be around for this event, but most of our children will be. It's important that your children are aware of this.

You will also be aware of some Top Secret government projects that they do not want the public to know. I have been fortunate over the years to have heard lectures from top-ranking government whistleblowers. I know things I am not supposed to know.

You need this information to take complete control of your life and to free your mind. The choice is yours. You can continue to remain a slave to our government or claim your freedom. **Choose wisely.**

Chapter 01

An Imminent Cosmic Event that will Change Your Life Forever

Warning: I know that most of you will find this difficult to believe and that you will be totally skeptical of this information which I can understand. It's perfectly legit to be skeptical. However, please know that the information I present comes from a higher source of consciousness. When this event occurs, your doubts will vanish in an instant. Those of us with a metaphysical background understand that this occurrence is imminent. I simply ask that you keep an open mind and consider the possibility that this could indeed happen.

This message is profoundly positive. A cosmic event is approaching, an imminent occurrence that will affect every individual on this planet. Yet only about ten percent of humanity is even aware of what is to come.

Every 13,000 years, precisely half of the precession of the equinox, a significant cosmic event unfolds in our solar system, profoundly impacting Earth and all forms of life. We are now reaching the end of another 13,000-year cycle. Few have studied the deeper history of our planet, but I have been fortunate to learn from enlightened teachers who have shared this knowledge.

It is part of human nature to forget. We have collectively lost the memory of what transpired 13,000 years ago when the great civilization of Atlantis sank beneath the oceans. This event has been recorded across nearly every ancient culture. The Vedas, Sumerian Tablets, Biblical texts, Egyptian writings, and the Mayan Codex all reference a global cataclysm. There have been five grand civilizations before the Great Flood, each achieving extraordinary levels of technology and spiritual understanding. But every one of them shared a tragic fate. Just as these civilizations reached the pinnacle of their evolution, a cataclysmic event erased them, obliterating their knowledge, progress, and treasures.

Although humanity during those ancient ages was advanced, they lacked the power to prevent their extinction. Today, however, messages received from higher divine sources, channeled by many, assure us that this time will be different. The coming transformation will not destroy humanity. Instead, we will experience what is known as the Grand Solar Flash.

So, what exactly is the Grand Solar Flash? It is an immensely powerful, Earth-directed solar flare unlike any seen before, an intense burst of magnetic white light from our Sun. Everyone on Earth will witness it. The intensity of this energy will trigger what is often called The Great Awakening, elevating the consciousness of all living beings. As the light floods our world, humanity's frequency will rise, initiating a profound and irreversible transformation.

This light, known as exotic gamma-level radiation or the light of the stars, has been scientifically shown to interact with DNA, instantly encoding it and evolving it to a higher level of complexity and functionality. The Grand Solar Flash, confirmed by a panel of historians and astronomers, is imminent. When the celestial bodies align in perfect formation, it will occur in the blink of an eye.

At that moment, we will transition to a higher vibrational state, a new version of Earth, radiant, peaceful, and filled with goodness. Those aligned with light and love energies will move forward into this higher realm, while those who cling to darkness or destructive intent will not survive the transition.

I know this may sound fantastical, yet it has been prophesied that the event could take place within the next thirty-five years. Only God knows the exact time. For further exploration, I recommend Michael Love's book *The Grand Solar Flash: The Event of a Lifetime*.

Author Ally Taylor has also shared valuable insights into this transformation. He writes:

"Earth is already in the process of transformation. The pandemic forced many to confront the importance of their decisions and the power

3 of the mind to manifest reality. We have become more aware of belief systems, societal conditioning, family influence, and mental health than ever before. Darkness is rising to the surface so that we may face it."

Taylor continues:

"The fifth dimension is imagination. Many people are beginning to access their creative gifts and apply them to life's challenges. Those who align with this new world will flourish, while those who resist it will remain behind. Humanity's consciousness is evolving from the third density to the fourth and ultimately the fifth, though all states exist simultaneously. Unfortunately, most remain anchored in third-dimensional awareness, unable to perceive anything beyond the limits of their senses, religion, government, and media. But human consciousness, like the ocean made of countless drops of water, is collective. As individual consciousness rises, the collective follows. The temperature of the sea of humanity will rise, and with it, our evolution. We do not simply arrive in higher dimensions; we expand into them. That is our soul's true journey."

Supporting this broader perspective, Dr. Nafeez Ahmed, a distinguished fellow at the Schumacher Institute for Sustainable Systems in the United Kingdom and author of a paper published in *Foresight Journal*, states that human civilization, now 8.2 billion strong, stands at a critical junction. According to Ahmed, we are teetering between two outcomes: authoritarian collapse or a new age of superabundance for all.

He explains that industrial civilization faces an inevitable decline, but this collapse could lead to the emergence of a post-materialist civilization built upon distributed, clean energy and new systems of cooperation. The challenge, he notes, lies in navigating the decline without allowing authoritarianism to dominate.

Ahmed identifies four stages in the life cycle of civilizations: growth, stability, decline, and transformation. He argues that humanity currently sits within the decline phase, but with the potential to transform if progress continues in renewable energy, artificial intelligence, 3D printing and lab-grown agriculture. These innovations could foster what he calls networked superabundance, where shared resources and technologies sustain global well-being without harming Earth's systems.

Gaya Herrington, a sustainability and systems analysis researcher at KPMG, agrees. In an interview with *The Independent*, she stated:

"We live in a historic now-or-never moment. What we do in the next five years will determine our well-being for the rest of this century."

This convergence of scientific insight and spiritual revelation suggests that humanity stands at a profound threshold. Whether guided by divine orchestration or cosmic cycles, we are being called to awaken, to rise in consciousness, and to participate in the transformation of our planet into a higher state of existence.

Chapter 02

The Doomsday Clock and the Cosmic Event

The Doomsday clock was just recently on the national news. Seventy-eight years ago, scientists created a unique sort of timepiece named the Doomsday Clock as a symbolic attempt to gauge how close humanity is to destroying the world. On Tuesday January 28, 2025 the clock was set at 89 seconds to midnight, the closest the world has ever been to that marker, according to the Bulletin of the Atomic Scientists, which established the clock in 1947. Midnight represents the moment at which people will have made the Earth uninhabitable.

The Doomsday Clock is a design that warns the public about how close we are to destroying our world with dangerous technologies of our own making. It is a metaphor, a reminder of the perils we must address if we are to survive on the planet. The Science and Security Board meet twice a year to discuss world events and reset the clock as necessary. The board is made up of scientists and other experts with deep knowledge of nuclear technology and climate science, who often provide expert advice to governments and international agencies. They consult widely with their colleagues across a range of disciplines and also seek the views of the *Bulletin*'s Board of Sponsors, which includes nine Nobel Laureates.

When the Doomsday Clock was created in 1947, the greatest danger to humanity came from nuclear weapons, in particular from the prospect that the United States and the Soviet Union were headed for a nuclear arms race. The *Bulletin* considered possible catastrophic disruptions from climate change in its hand-setting deliberations for the first time in 2007.

In 2025, the Science and Security Board set the time to 89 seconds to midnight because, despite unmistakable signs of danger, national leaders and their societies failed to do what is needed to change course. We set the clock closer to midnight because we do not see sufficient, positive progress on the global challenges we face, including nuclear risk, climate change, biological threats and advances in disruptive technologies" such as artificial intelligence, said Daniel Holz, the Bulletin's science and security board chair and professor in the department of physics, astronomy and astrophysics at the University of Chicago, in a news briefing Tuesday. "The countries that possess nuclear weapons are increasing the size and role of their arsenals, investing hundreds of billions of dollars in weapons that can destroy civilization many times over."

Over the last 78 years, the clock's time has changed according to how close scientists believe the human race is to total destruction. Some years the time changes, and some years it doesn't. The Doomsday Clock is set every year by experts on the Bulletin's Science and Security Board in consultation with its Board of Sponsors, which was first established by Albert Einstein in December 1948, with J. Robert_Oppenheimer as its first chair. The board currently includes nine Nobel laureates, many of them in physics, physiology or medicine. The clock has been an effective wake-up call when it comes to reminding people about the cascading crises the planet is facing.

However, God in his divine wisdom is fully aware of what is happening on our planet. Even though scientists are aware of this alarming clock, they have no knowledge whatsoever of the Cosmic Event. This Cosmic Event is going to occur in divine order at exactly the right time. You need to have faith and trust in our Heavenly Father. I hope all of you will trust in God knowing that miracles can happen for this event is truly a miracle.

Chapter 03

Key Metaphysical Concepts That Have the Potential to Alter Your Life

The field of metaphysics possesses the concepts that answer some of the most basic questions such as "Why am I here?", "Where did I come from?", "Who am I?" and one of the biggest questions is "What is my purpose in being here?". I have researched and studied the metaphysical realm for over 30 years and yes it has greatly enhanced my life. The following are major concepts that I have learned over the years that explains our existence. I hope these concepts will also assist you in making your life better and more successful. Some of you will already have incorporated these concepts into your life.

The very first concept is *"There are no coincidences in your life"*. Everything in your life happens for a reason. Unfortunately, the vast majority of the time we have no clue about the reason until later in life.

There's a reason why certain people are in your life now. This idea connects to the concept of reincarnation. I understand that only about a third to half of people believe in reincarnation. From my research, I have learned that in 553 A.D., during the Second Council of Constantinople, the concept of reincarnation was removed from the Bible. I believe this occurred because reincarnation teaches personal responsibility for one's spiritual evolution. You do not need to rely on religion alone to reach higher states of being. In my view, religion provides a foundation, a set of guiding principles, but at some point, we must go beyond dogma and pursue our own understanding through direct experience and self-discovery.

Another belief I hold is that Jesus was not solely a savior but rather a master teacher. I know this may challenge traditional views, but it is through living and applying his teachings that we experience transformation. The people in our lives today are often souls we have known before, and the unresolved issues between us are opportunities for growth. In this sense, there are no coincidences, only meaningful encounters meant to help us evolve.

If you are intrigued by this subject, I highly recommend *Reincarnation Handbook: Techniques of Past Life Regression* by Robert and Loy Young. I had the privilege of meeting both of them and attending several of their lectures.

One of the most fascinating stories they shared involved a woman they regressed to a past life in seventeenth-century France. This woman, who had never left New England, described being six years old and visiting a cathedral with her parents. She recalled a cornerstone at the base of the building with a specific date and a French inscription. Intrigued, Robert and Loy later traveled to France to investigate. The bishop of the cathedral told them there was no cornerstone as far as he knew. Still, with his permission, they dug near the spot the woman had described and, to everyone's astonishment, found the stone exactly as she had recounted it, complete with the date and inscription. This is just one of many examples that suggest reincarnation may indeed be part of our spiritual reality.

Being born on Mother Earth is analogous to enrolling in a major University. Before you were born, you as a soul essence had a conference with your guardian angel and spirit guides to design a blueprint for your life. We decide where we will be born, who our parents will be, and what experiences we will encounter. Many people wonder why they would choose difficult parents or challenging circumstances. The answer, I believe, is that these experiences offer the greatest opportunities for learning and spiritual advancement. Often, our parents and closest relationships are souls with whom we have shared previous lifetimes. Our guardian angels and guides are always nearby, ready to assist us, but they will never interfere without our consent. Because we live in a universe governed by free will, they cannot act unless we ask for their help. Once we have learned the lessons we came here to master, we are free to move beyond the cycle of reincarnation.

Since we live in a free will universe, we can alter or refine our life plans at any time. Earth, as I see it, is a school for the soul, where we choose the lessons that will help us grow. Unfortunately, many people live by what I call default values, beliefs passed down by parents, schools, or governments, without questioning them. These inherited values can limit our spiritual progress. It is essential to remember that each of us possesses divine power and creative potential given by our Creator. The key to reclaiming this power lies in one simple truth: the power of love.

Another fact that may surprise many is that most people possess some level of psychic ability. Research supports this idea. A study published in the Journal of the American Society for Psychical Research found that approximately fifty three percent of Americans have experienced at least one psychic or paranormal event. These include extrasensory perception, out of body experiences, contact with the deceased, memories of past lives, encounters with apparitions, prophetic dreams, or experiences in haunted places. The study was conducted by the Parapsychology Division of the University of Virginia School of Medicine, which surveyed both students and adults in Charlottesville, Virginia.

One of the most empowering metaphysical principles I have learned is that our beliefs, combined with our emotions, shape our reality. Whatever we focus on consistently will manifest in our lives. The key word here is "consistently." Our minds function much like computers. If we feed them negativity, we will receive negative outcomes. We must become vigilant gatekeepers of our thoughts, filtering out destructive beliefs and reinforcing positive ones. In this analogy, the mind is the software, and the brain is the hardware.

Another concept that has transformed my understanding of spiritual growth is what mystics call "The Dark Night of the Soul." This term describes a period of deep spiritual crisis, times when we may feel lost, abandoned, or disconnected from the divine. Though painful, this stage is an essential part of transformation. It strips away illusions, ego attachments, and false beliefs, making room for a truer connection with our higher self. Symptoms of the Dark Night of the Soul often include sadness, emptiness, confusion, and even physical fatigue. In my experience, this phase arises when the soul is calling us back to our authentic nature. It is not a random misfortune but a sacred intervention meant to awaken us. This process can be triggered by loss, illness, or major life transitions.

When we emerge from this dark night, we are not the same. We are reborn with a deeper understanding, renewed purpose, and a stronger connection to love and truth. The duration of this experience varies, sometimes lasting days, months, or even years, but it always serves a divine purpose. Each time we pass through it, we move closer to enlightenment and spiritual freedom.

Chapter 04

Recent Message from Gaia

It saddens me deeply that so many people remain unaware of the living presence of our divine Mother Earth, who has both a soul and consciousness. She is aware of all that takes place within and upon her. Her true name is Gaia.

Marianne Vaughn, a highly respected psychic, is cherished by all beings of light for her profound healing energy and the guidance she offers to others. With her permission, I share the message she recently received from Gaia herself.

"Hello, dear one. I am so happy you have connected with me in this way. You and I are joined at the heart, and that makes it easy for me to share my thoughts with you. How do I feel about the Ascension happening now? It is intense; it is a lot to experience. I am a soul just like all of you, and this is not an easy time. It is not, as you say, a bowl of cherries."

"These times are hard, but they are also extraordinary. You often compare this moment to the transition that occurs during human childbirth, and I would agree. It is messy and painful, yet the gift is coming. The most difficult period for me was long ago when very few people cared about my well-being. Humanity lacked the awareness to see that I was a living being like them. That was the time when whales were slaughtered without compassion, when the destructive power of the bomb was unleashed, when cruelty and ignorance defined the past. It has been a long history of harm done without conscious thought."

"But these times are different. Many hearts now know that I am alive, and many hearts care. Not all hearts, of course, for some are wounded and locked in pain, but love is here now. These are the first stirrings of the Aquarian Age. My beloved beings from the Devic Realm have been called into service to help cleanse and heal my body. This process brings great pain to my plants and animals, but it is necessary for me to carry my light and continue to ascend. Still, it hurts. That is why your love, light, and the codes you carry are so precious to me."

"You and the many others who care about me are helping me to heal. I know that you are all concerned about the broken masculine system that has caused so much imbalance. This mindset, which has ignored my well-being for thousands of years, is finally being revealed. The strength of the feminine energy is now rising, bringing balance to me once more. Yes, the turmoil is difficult, but it is part of the painful transition that will give birth to something beautiful and new."

"Anything you are guided to do to help me is deeply appreciated, whether it is sending energy, signing petitions, or supporting organizations that protect my body. I feel it all. Love will triumph in the end. This is certain, and I know it with all my being. I am bathed in the light being sent to me, and although the road ahead may be bumpy for a while, we will make it through together. I send you so much love for knowing me, for loving me, and for being a voice that carries my vibration to others. Your light is a gift, and I love you for it. Together, we will rise.

In eternal love,

Gaia

Chapter 05

The Power of the Subconscious Mind and How to Reprogram It

Everything in existence vibrates at a certain frequency, from the smallest atom to the farthest galaxy. This includes not only physical matter but also our thoughts, emotions, and beliefs. Every thought you hold emits a vibration, and the stronger the emotion attached to that thought, the more powerful its vibration becomes. From the moment we are born, before our conscious mind begins to form and filter experiences, all the information we receive from our parents, caregivers, and surroundings flows directly into the subconscious mind. By the age of five, these impressions have created a foundation of beliefs and perceptions stored within what I call the paradigm—a mental framework through which we interpret reality.

This paradigm is not static; it is built and reinforced through repetition. Society, education systems, media, and even governments play a significant role in shaping and solidifying these patterns. From an early age, we are conditioned to conform, to obey, and to accept authority without question. As Albert Einstein wisely observed, "Blind belief in authority is the greatest enemy of truth." Most people grow up unaware that their daily thoughts, decisions, and emotional reactions are influenced by deeply rooted programs that were never consciously chosen.

The paradigms stored within the subconscious mind determine the vibrations we emit. These vibrations, in turn, guide our actions, shape our relationships, and ultimately define the results we experience in life. Habits, beliefs, and emotional responses are all components of this inner structure. Our emotions serve as signals—our conscious awareness of the vibrations we are currently resonating with. The thoughts we consistently focus on either strengthen the existing paradigm or begin to rewire it.

The people and circumstances we attract into our lives are not random; they align with our dominant frequencies. This is why it is crucial to consciously choose the influences around us. To reprogram the subconscious for success, we must protect it from negative energy. The subconscious mind is like fertile soil—it will grow whatever seeds are planted in it, whether they are thoughts of fear, doubt, and limitation, or thoughts of faith, confidence, and abundance. Constant exposure to negativity from news, gossip, toxic relationships, or social media can quietly shape your beliefs, limit your self-image, and lower your vibration.

As I began the journey of reprogramming my own mind, I discovered a simple yet profound truth: proximity is power. The people and environments we surround ourselves with either elevate us or drain us. Seek out those who uplift you, challenge you to grow, and reflect the qualities you aspire to embody. Fill your days with books that inspire, music that soothes and strengthens, and films or content that expand your sense of what's possible. Over time, this consistent exposure transforms your subconscious mind, allowing it to become your ally rather than your obstacle.

Your subconscious mind holds the master key to your success and well-being. It governs your core beliefs, values, and emotional patterns. It decides what information to make conscious and what to suppress. It influences every decision, every action, and every perception of reality—often operating silently in the background. To truly change your life, you must learn to work with this inner powerhouse rather than against it.

Reprogramming the subconscious is a gradual process—it typically takes about three to four weeks of consistent effort to begin seeing noticeable changes, although deeply ingrained patterns may take longer. The subconscious does not differentiate between what is real and what is imagined; it responds only to repetition and emotion. This is why affirmations, visualization, and self-hypnosis can be so effective when practiced with genuine feeling. The subconscious mind is immensely more powerful than the conscious mind—it influences not just behavior but also perception, creativity, and even logic itself.

If you are not achieving the results you desire, it may be time to examine your inner programming. Begin by setting a clear intention— a focused, emotionally charged desire that acts as an electromagnetic signal you send out into the universe. The universe, in turn, mirrors that energy back to you through experiences, opportunities, and synchronicities. The more emotion and attention you invest in your intention, the stronger and faster the reflection will be.

The greatest mistake most people make in this process is giving up too soon. The law of manifestation requires patience and faith. Persistence is the fuel that keeps your intentions alive even when there is no visible progress. You may hold a vision for weeks, months, or even years, only to see everything align in an instant. Know that as long as your intention remains strong, it continues to work silently behind the scenes.

Remember, emotion is energy in motion. The deeper you feel about a goal, the more power you give it. Choose intentions that ignite passion within you, that truly matter to your heart and soul. When your frequency rises, your manifestations accelerate. Physical matter itself is simply energy condensed into form; it takes time for thoughts to materialize in the physical world. On higher planes of existence, manifestation is instantaneous because vibration is lighter and more fluid. But here, in the physical realm, patience, consistency, and emotional alignment are essential.

If you wish to enhance your ability to manifest consciously, explore methods that help you access and reprogram your subconscious mind. One highly effective tool is *Deliberate Creation Instant Self-Hypnosis* by Dr. Robert Anthony, along with other guided self-hypnosis recordings available online. These resources can help align your subconscious beliefs with your conscious desires, bridging the gap between thought and reality.

The key to transformation lies within. The universe does not respond to what you want—it responds to what you are. As you elevate your vibration through awareness, intention, and emotional mastery, life begins to reflect that change in ways that seem almost miraculous. The power has always been within you; it simply awaits your conscious command.

Here are three steps that have personally helped me reprogram my mind:

Step One: Decide Clarity is the foundation of transformation. Decide exactly what you want and visualize it in detail. The clearer your vision, the more powerful it becomes. Wherever your focus goes, your energy flows. Decide to move beyond where you are and create the life you truly desire.

Step Two: Commit Commit fully to overcoming negativity. Commit to your growth and to your higher path. True commitment means cutting off all other possibilities. When you give yourself fully to change, you rise to new levels of strength and determination.

Step Three: Resolve Once you have decided and committed, take inspired action. Evaluate what works and what does not. Resolve is about adaptability and perseverance. When you encounter a roadblock, find another way forward. Life rarely follows a straight line. Every obstacle is an opportunity to grow stronger and more creative.

As long as you keep moving forward, you are on the right path. The true power lies within you. Reprogramming your subconscious may bring unexpected challenges, but each one holds the potential for a breakthrough. Every setback can become a step forward when viewed through the lens of persistence and faith.

That is the power of resolve, the power of the mind, and ultimately, the power of creation itself.

Chapter 06

The Power of Prayer

I have learned through both experience and research that prayer is one of the most powerful tools available to us. Time and time again, it has been shown to create real and lasting change. You can choose to ask God, or whoever you believe your creator is, for assistance in helping you to detach from all negative energies that surround you, or you could implement your own program to install into your subconscious mind.

When I pray, I choose to ask God, or the divine source I believe in, to help me detach from any negative energies that surround me. Sometimes, instead of praying in words, I also use techniques that work directly with my subconscious mind to replace negative patterns with positive ones.

As I mentioned earlier, there are countless CDs and MP3s that can assist with this kind of inner work. I find it helpful to use them regularly because the world around us is filled with negativity. We absorb so much of it every day—through the media, through conversations, and sometimes even from those closest to us. There have been times when I have had to stop watching the news altogether because I could feel how its negativity was affecting my energy and thoughts. I have also noticed that negativity can come from neighbors, friends, or even strangers.

That is why it is essential for me to protect my mind and spirit. I make a conscious effort to filter what I allow into my awareness. Prayer is a form of that protection, a way of cleansing and strengthening the mind against anything that does not serve love or growth.

Now, I realize what I am about to say may challenge some people's beliefs, but I speak from my own understanding. I believe that Jesus was not meant to be seen as a savior in the traditional sense. Please allow me to explain. It is our personal responsibility to save ourselves through conscious choice and inner transformation. Jesus was, in truth, a master teacher—just like Buddha, Muhammad, and Krishna.

The real salvation comes from living according to the lessons these enlightened beings shared. When we embody their teachings—when we live with compassion, forgiveness, and awareness—we naturally align ourselves with divine truth. That alignment is what brings salvation. And for those who may not know, Jesus is now known by his true name, Sananda. If you would like to receive current messages from Jesus, just Google "Channeled Messages from Sananda-aka Jesus.

Chapter 07

Lessons from Quantum Physics

This next concept is difficult for many people to grasp, but I have come to understand that we are living in an illusionary world. Quantum physics has revealed this truth beyond a shadow of a doubt. At the quantum level, reality does not exist unless it is being observed. This was proven through the famous double-slit experiment.

Albert Einstein once said, "Reality is merely an illusion, albeit a very persistent one." Those words have always stayed with me because they confirm what quantum physics continues to show us: that what we call physical reality is not as solid as it seems.

Scientists agree that an atom is about ninety-nine percent space. Considering that the human body contains roughly seven octillion atoms—about seven times ten to the twenty-seventh power—our physical form is almost entirely made of empty space. That means what we perceive as solid matter is, in truth, an illusion. So why do we feel physical? That question is far more complex than it appears, and I do not pretend to have all the answers. I simply offer this idea for contemplation. It helps us begin to understand what Einstein meant about living in an illusory world.

Insights from the CIA's Declassified Documents

The next few ideas come directly from declassified documents from the CIA. The first major point those documents make is that physical matter does not actually exist—everything that appears solid is, in fact, energy.

According to the same documents, the universe and the human mind are holograms. They describe reality as a vast, interacting field of energy—some in motion and some at rest—forming one immense and complex hologram. The human mind, also a hologram, aligns with the universal hologram through energy exchange. This interaction produces meaning and creates the state we call consciousness.

The CIA's findings also suggest that human consciousness can enter new realms of awareness. Between the absolute, infinite energy outside our dimension and the material universe we perceive, there are multiple intervening dimensions. Through altered states of consciousness, the human mind can begin to access these dimensions. For this to happen, consciousness must focus so coherently that its frequency allows perception beyond time and space.

One of the programs designed to explore this idea was known as the Gateway Experience. When used patiently and systematically, it was said to help human consciousness create coherent patterns of awareness in these higher dimensions.

Another revelation from these documents is that time is not linear. It exists as a field where the past, present, and future all occur simultaneously. This means that human consciousness, when sufficiently focused, can access information from any point in time. These conclusions echo what Einstein taught us about the nature of time itself.

Understanding True Reality

I bring all this up because if our physical reality is an illusion, then through the power of our minds, we can reshape that illusion into whatever form we wish to experience. That raises an important question: what is true reality?

True reality begins in the fifth dimension and beyond—the realm of the soul. In the fifth dimension, energies of love and light prevail. There is no war, no hatred, no racism, and nothing of a negative nature. Our purpose, as I understand it, is to rise to that level of existence by letting go of fear and everything that feeds negativity, and by spreading love throughout the world.

There are higher dimensions beyond the fifth—some sources suggest at least twelve. Each one vibrates at a higher frequency than the one below it. But for now, our focus should be on reaching the fifth dimension, for that is where true transformation begins.

The Unity of All Consciousness

Perhaps the most profound truth of all is that everything in existence is interconnected. Beneath the illusion of separation, we are all threads woven into the same cosmic fabric—expressions of one infinite consciousness. Through this collective consciousness, we are one. Every thought, emotion, and action we direct toward another ultimately reverberates back to us, for there is no true division between "you" and "me." This principle lies at the heart of karma, a universal law that transcends culture, religion, and philosophy. It is echoed in sacred texts across the ages, including the Bible's timeless wisdom: *"What you sow is what you reap."* Even modern science reflects this truth through Newton's Third Law of Motion—*for every action, there is an equal and opposite reaction.*

If humanity genuinely understood and lived by this awareness, the world would be transformed. There would be no wars born of fear and greed, no racism rooted in ignorance, and no violence born of separation. Compassion and cooperation would replace conflict and division. Peace would not need to be enforced; it would arise naturally, the inevitable expression of an awakened collective mind.

Quantum physics has begun to bridge the gap between spirituality and science, revealing that we are not isolated physical beings but energetic expressions of a unified field—one vast, intelligent consciousness that connects every particle in existence. Each thought, each emotion, each intention sends ripples through this quantum field, influencing not only our personal reality but also the shared human experience.

This understanding means that we are infinitely more powerful than we have been led to believe. The energy we emit—whether through love, gratitude, or fear—returns to us in the same form. When we radiate kindness, it comes back multiplied. When we project anger or judgment, that too finds its way back, sometimes instantly, sometimes after years, but always in perfect balance with the energy we sent forth. This is not punishment; it is universal harmony in motion.

Every act of love uplifts not just the giver and the receiver, but all of humanity. Every thought of forgiveness lightens the collective burden of pain. Every expression of gratitude raises the vibration of the planet. When we begin to see ourselves as integral parts of one living, breathing consciousness, our choices shift. We become more mindful, more compassionate, and more aware that what we put into the world is what we ultimately live within.

To live by this truth is to participate consciously in the evolution of the human spirit—to move from separation to unity, from fear to love, from reaction to creation. The more we understand our connection to the universal mind, the more we realize that by healing ourselves, we heal the world. And when we send love into the universe, it always finds its way back—because in truth, there is nowhere else for it to go.

Chapter 08

The Most Complicated Concept in Quantum Physics

One of the most mysterious and profound subjects within quantum physics is the concept of time itself. Unlike the straightforward progression we perceive in daily life, time is not linear. It does not flow neatly from past to present to future as our minds are conditioned to believe. As several declassified CIA documents have also suggested, time operates more like an infinite web of simultaneous realities—each timeline existing parallel to the others, each influencing and intersecting with the rest in subtle yet powerful ways.

Albert Einstein once articulated this beautifully when he said, "Time is basically an illusion created by the mind to aid in our sense of temporal presence in the vast ocean of space." His insight captures an essential truth: time, as we experience it, is a construct of consciousness. It allows us to navigate existence in an orderly fashion, yet beyond our limited perception, everything is happening now—every possibility, every version of reality unfolding at once within the boundless continuum of the quantum field.

One of the most intriguing explorations of this concept came from a covert study known as **Project Looking Glass**, conducted by the CIA. The project sought to understand how human consciousness interacts with potential futures and how individuals might respond to certain events or manipulative programs across different timelines. The results, as described in various reports, were astonishing. By 2012, researchers claimed that all possible timelines were converging into two distinct trajectories—one reflecting a path of positive evolution and awakening, and the other embodying fear, division, and regression.

This revelation reportedly caused deep concern among those in positions of power, for it implied that beyond a certain threshold, no human or technological interference could alter the inevitable unfolding of events. The convergence indicated that humanity had reached a pivotal point in its spiritual and energetic development—a collective crossroads where consciousness itself would determine the direction of our future.

Though Project Looking Glass was said to have been shut down, its implications remain profoundly thought-provoking. It suggested that reality is not fixed but fluid, shaped continuously by collective vibration and intention. Humanity, it seemed, was standing on the edge of a massive energetic shift, a bifurcation of timelines that would lead either toward unity, love, and enlightenment or toward chaos, control, and disconnection.

This idea aligns closely with what many spiritual teachers, mystics, and even quantum theorists have long proposed: that our thoughts and emotions do not merely exist within time; they create it. Each choice, each belief, and each vibration contributes to the unfolding of a specific version of reality. The timelines we experience are, in essence, mirrors of our collective consciousness.

If the reports are to be believed, then the convergence of timelines in 2012 was not the end of the world as some feared, but rather the beginning of a new phase in human evolution, a shift from passive existence to conscious creation. It was the moment when humanity began to awaken to its own power as the architect of reality.

Perhaps the real lesson of Project Looking Glass is not about secret technology or classified experiments, but about the realization that we are the experiment. Time bends and weaves around our awareness, responding to the energy we emit. And as our collective vibration rises, we continue to move toward the timeline of higher consciousness, one defined by compassion, wisdom, and the understanding that we are not prisoners of time, but its creators.

Chapter 09

Project Pegasus

Another story that I find intriguing is that of Andrew D. Basiago, a lawyer from Vancouver, Washington. He holds six academic qualifications including degrees from UCLA and Cambridge. He claims to have participated as a child in a secret U.S. government project known as Project Pegasus, which allegedly explored time travel and teleportation under the Defense Advanced Research Projects Agency.

Basiago is said to have been one of several "chrononauts"—time travelers—trained to test the effects of temporal movement on the human body and mind. He also asserts that teleportation and time travel technologies were developed decades ago, but have been withheld from public use. It is estimated that his IQ is around 195, which is one of the highest IQs in the world.

His claims are supported by Alfred Webre, a lawyer specializing in exopolitics, who believes these technologies could revolutionize how humanity connects and communicates. Basiago also attributes much of this technology to research derived from the late inventor Nikola Tesla.

Chapter 10

Parallel Universes

Finally, I want to explore one of the most fascinating and mind-expanding ideas in both science and philosophy—the concept of parallel universes, often referred to as the multiverse. This theory first emerged in the 1950s, when Hugh Everett, a brilliant Princeton physicist, introduced it as part of his doctoral dissertation. I first encountered Everett's groundbreaking work many years ago through a PBS documentary that delved into the nature of reality and consciousness. His theory proposed something truly revolutionary: that every possible outcome of every decision, action, or event actually occurs—but in separate, coexisting universes.

According to Everett's Many-Worlds Interpretation, when a decision is made or a quantum event takes place, reality doesn't collapse into one single outcome; rather, it branches into countless versions of itself. Every possible scenario exists somewhere in the infinite expanse of parallel dimensions. Over the years, this once-controversial idea has gained increasing recognition, supported by prominent thinkers such as Stephen Hawking and Elon Musk, who have both publicly acknowledged their belief in the multiverse. Today, many quantum physicists and cosmologists seriously entertain the notion that our universe is but one of many—an infinite collection of realities, each governed by the same universal principles but differing in outcomes, experiences, and evolution.

To me, this concept is both humbling and empowering. It reminds us that we are not confined to a single linear experience of existence. Infinite versions of reality unfold simultaneously, shaped by the endless choices made by consciousness itself. It suggests that the self is not bound to one timeline, but rather connected through awareness to an infinite spectrum of possibilities. Consciousness may very well be the bridge that links all universes, observing and interacting with different realities depending on frequency and vibrational alignment.

This perspective gives profound meaning to the choices we make and the thoughts we hold. Every decision sends ripples through creation, influencing not only our personal path but also the direction of infinite parallel selves exploring other outcomes. In essence, the multiverse reminds us of our infinite potential—to grow, to evolve, and to manifest new realities through the power of awareness.

Chapter 11

The Law of Entropy

There is another principle—one that operates in both the physical and societal realms—that profoundly shapes our world: **The Law of Entropy**. Surprisingly, very few people understand how deeply this law affects their lives. Rooted in the Second Law of Thermodynamics, it states that in an isolated system, the total entropy—a measure of disorder or randomness—always increases over time. In other words, everything in the universe naturally tends toward chaos and disintegration unless external energy or effort is applied to maintain order.

Entropy is not just a scientific abstraction—it is a universal truth that governs all things, from the smallest atom to the largest galaxy, from personal relationships to entire civilizations. In practical terms, anything that requires work or structure inevitably releases some energy into its surroundings, resulting in gradual decay or inefficiency. Without consistent care, focus, and renewal, systems break down. This is as true for machines and buildings as it is for governments and human societies.

President Thomas Jefferson, the Father of the U.S. Constitution, captured this truth with striking accuracy when he said, "Experience hath shown, that even under the best forms of government, those entrusted with power have, in time, and by slow operations, perverted it into tyranny." His words mirror the essence of the Second Law of

Thermodynamics. Over time, even the most well-intentioned institutions, if left unchecked, deteriorate into disorder and corruption unless renewed by conscious effort, reform, and accountability.

We can observe the Law of Entropy in our everyday lives. Take your home, for example. Without regular maintenance, cleaning, and care, it will inevitably decay—paint fades, structures weaken, and systems fail. The same applies to your physical body, your relationships, your work, and even your spiritual practice. Without the consistent infusion of energy—through love, attention, and action—everything drifts toward disorder.

Our food supply offers another striking example. Over the years, the quality and vitality of our food have declined due to over-processing, depletion of soil nutrients, and the widespread use of chemicals. This, too, is entropy in action—the gradual breakdown of natural order into artificial, less vital forms.

The Law of Entropy is, in essence, a call to awareness. It reminds us that nothing sustains itself automatically. Order, growth, and harmony require continual renewal—an investment of conscious energy. In the same way that the universe trends toward disorder, so too do our thoughts, societies, and institutions when we cease to nurture them with wisdom and integrity.

Recognizing this truth empowers us to take responsibility—not only for maintaining our physical surroundings but also for preserving the order within our own minds and hearts. Just as entropy governs the 37 physical world, consciousness holds the power to reverse it. Through awareness, intention, and the consistent infusion of positive energy, we can bring structure back to chaos and elevate our reality to a higher, more harmonious vibration.

Chapter 12

The Mandela Effect

Another fascinating and often controversial topic worth exploring is what has come to be known as **"The Mandela Effect."** Many of you may already be familiar with the term. Officially, according to government and mainstream scientific explanations, the Mandela Effect describes a phenomenon in which a large group of people collectively misremembers a historical event, quote, or fact. The term was first coined by writer and researcher **Fiona Broome** over a decade ago, after she created a website recounting her vivid memories of former South African President **Nelson Mandela** dying in prison during the 1980s. However, according to the official historical record, Mandela passed away on **December 5, 2013**, long after his release from prison and subsequent presidency.

The government and conventional science insist that this phenomenon can be explained through cognitive psychology—faulty memory, confabulation, or social reinforcement. Yet, for those who have personally experienced it, the Mandela Effect cannot be dismissed so easily. The truth is that a significant number of people—possibly millions—share identical memories of events that no longer match the current reality. These individuals, myself included, have no clear explanation for why our recollections differ so precisely and consistently from the "official" version of history.

Skeptics label it as false memory, but I ask you: what are the odds that **millions of people across different cultures and countries** would all misremember the same details in the exact same way? For those of us who have experienced this shift, it feels as though we have somehow crossed into a different timeline—a slightly altered version of reality where small but undeniable differences exist. Those who were not affected cannot truly comprehend it, just as those of us who were affected cannot fully explain why it happened.

Take, for instance, one of the most famous examples—the legendary line from **Star Wars: Episode V – The Empire Strikes Back (1980)**. Ask nearly anyone what Darth Vader said to Luke Skywalker during that iconic moment, and they will tell you, *"Luke, I am your father."* Yet, in this current timeline, the line has become, *"No, I am your father."* The change seems small, but it's unmistakable. Even more curious, last year I watched an interview clip of **James Earl Jones**, the actor who voiced Darth Vader, where he distinctly said, "I know what I said. I said, 'Luke, I am your father.'"

Another example is found in the timeless film **Casablanca (1942).** For decades, movie lovers remembered **Ingrid Bergman's** character, Ilsa, saying, *"Play it again, Sam."* The phrase became one of the most quoted lines in cinema history. Yet, if you watch the film today, she never says those exact words. Instead, she says, *"Play it, Sam."* I personally recall hearing the former version vividly, and so do countless others who watched the movie years ago.

Then there's **Snow White and the Seven Dwarfs (1937)**. As children, most of us remember the Evil Queen gazing into her mirror and saying, *"Mirror, mirror on the wall, who's the fairest of them all?"* But in this timeline, the phrase has inexplicably changed to, *"Magic mirror on the wall."* Again, the question arises: why would millions of people around the world share the same collective memory that no longer aligns with recorded reality?

Another classic example is the television show once known as **Sex in the City**. Many people—including myself—distinctly remember it that way. Yet, in the present timeline, the official title has always been **Sex and the City**. Strangely enough, episodes of *The Big Bang Theory* have characters referring to it as Sex in the City, confirming that even mainstream media once acknowledged this version.

Even the beloved line from **Forrest Gump (1994)** seems to have shifted. The famous quote so many of us remember is, *"Life is like a box of chocolates."* But if you watch the film today, the line has become, *"Life was like a box of chocolates."* The past tense "was" feels completely unnatural and inconsistent with the original sentiment of the film.

These examples—and there are many more—leave us with profound questions about memory, consciousness, and the nature of reality itself. Could it be that consciousness is not merely a passive observer of the universe, but an active participant capable of shifting between parallel timelines? Could our collective awareness occasionally "jump" into alternate versions of history where details have changed ever so slightly?

Skeptics may continue to dismiss the Mandela Effect as a quirk of human memory, but for those of us who remember differently, the experience is far too consistent and widespread to ignore. Whether it represents a psychological anomaly, a dimensional shift, or evidence of a multiverse interacting with our consciousness, one thing remains clear—the Mandela Effect challenges our very understanding of time, perception, and reality itself.

So I ask only this: do not accuse those who have experienced it of misremembering. Our memories are not illusions. They are fragments of timelines we once inhabited—proof, perhaps, that reality is far more fluid and mysterious than most dare to believe.

Chapter 13

The Power of Forgiveness

The law of forgiveness is one of the hardest yet most important laws to learn. Forgiveness is not something that comes naturally to most of us, especially when someone we trusted has betrayed or hurt us in ways that leave lasting emotional scars. The pain can run so deep that even thinking about the person can stir anger, resentment, or sadness. Yet true healing cannot begin until forgiveness takes root. It is not about excusing their actions or forgetting what happened; it is about freeing yourself from the emotional prison that pain creates.

When someone in your life has deeply hurt you and caused you great suffering, forgiveness is never an easy task. You need to allow yourself the space to feel every emotion such as anger, grief, disappointment, and confusion. Suppressing these emotions will only cause them to resurface in other ways. Taking time to sit with your pain and understand it is the first step toward releasing it. Forgiveness begins not with the other person but within yourself, when you decide that you no longer wish to carry the burden of that pain.

One method I have found helpful is to write a letter to the person who hurt you. Pour your heart into that letter. Describe in as much detail as possible what they did, how it made you feel, and how their actions affected your life. Do not hold back; let your emotions flow onto the paper, no matter how raw or uncomfortable they may be. When you have expressed everything that needs to be said, sign your name at the end. This act of writing becomes a form of emotional release, an acknowledgment of the pain that you have carried. end. This act of writing becomes a form of emotional release, an acknowledgment of the pain that you have carried.

The next step is not to send the letter but to gently set it alight and let it burn completely. As the paper turns to ash, imagine the emotional weight lifting from your heart. Feel the release. As it burns, say to yourself, "I now release to the heavens all the negative energy associated with this person and my pain." Then speak their name and affirm with conviction, "You are now completely forgiven." In that moment, you reclaim your power and choose peace over bitterness. You are not doing this for them; you are doing it for yourself.

Forgiveness is not a single act but a process. You may find old feelings of anger or resentment resurfacing from time to time. When they do, remind yourself that forgiveness is an ongoing journey. Each time you consciously release those emotions, you weaken their hold over you. Over time, you will find the memories no longer sting the way they once did. What once brought you sorrow may eventually bring wisdom and strength.

Because we are all connected through consciousness, that connection remains until forgiveness is truly given. Energetically, we are bound to those with whom we share strong emotions, whether positive or negative. Holding on to resentment keeps that energetic tie alive, draining your peace and vitality. True forgiveness severs that unhealthy connection and restores balance to your spirit.

Remember, all thoughts are energy. The more emotion you invest in a thought, the stronger that energy becomes. When you dwell on anger or revenge, you feed that energy and it continues to shape your life in unseen ways. But when you choose forgiveness, you shift that energy toward love, healing, and renewal. Forgiveness is the key that unlocks emotional freedom; it opens the door for peace, compassion, and growth to enter your life once again.

Chapter 14

The Illusional Concept of Death

It simply amazes me that so many people live in fear of death when, in truth, death itself is a complete illusion. Humanity has long misunderstood this natural process, seeing it as an ending rather than a transformation. Yet countless stories from every corner of the world tell a very different story. They speak of consciousness continuing beyond the body, of awareness expanding into realms that words can barely describe. These are not the fantasies of hopeful minds; they are lived experiences from people who have clinically died and returned to tell what lies beyond the veil.

People need to understand that we were created as pure soul essence. The body is not who we truly are. It is merely a temporary vehicle, a vessel that allows our soul to navigate the density of the third-dimensional world. Just as we step out of a car when we reach our destination, so too does the soul step out of the body when its earthly journey is complete. Death, therefore, is not a failure or a punishment; it is simply a transition from one state of being to another.

The following is a true story of a near-death experience that beautifully illustrates this truth. Adam Tapp, a professional paramedic, once died for more than eleven minutes after being accidentally electrocuted during a woodworking project. During that time, he experienced something that forever changed his understanding of life and death.

Tapp recalled that the moment his physical body stopped functioning, he felt a wave of absolute tranquility wash over him. There was no pain, no fear, and no confusion—only peace. "I felt like I was falling for ages," he said, "and then it was just like waking up from a nap somewhere that I'd always been." He described seeing not through eyes but through awareness itself, observing everything from a single point that extended infinitely in all directions. "I was seeing spherically from a single point outward, like I had just become a single point of awareness. I wasn't dead. I wasn't anything—just perfect, absolute contentment."

In that realm beyond time, Tapp felt himself merge with what he called the very fabric of the universe. There was no sense of separation between himself and everything else. He became part of the energy that sustains all creation, where every thought and vibration flowed in perfect harmony. He later said the experience was not frightening but profoundly natural, as if returning home after a long journey.

When doctors finally managed to restart his heart, Tapp's soul was drawn back into his physical form. He remained in a coma for eight hours, suspended between two realities. When he finally awoke in the hospital, he had no understanding of how much time had passed. The world around him felt unfamiliar, as if he were seeing it for the first time.

In the days that followed, he described feeling acutely aware of his body and surroundings. At first, he felt detached, as though life itself were a dream, but over time he found acceptance and peace. The experience left him certain that consciousness does not end with death. It merely shifts its focus, continuing its journey in another form.

Stories like Adam Tapp's remind us that death is not something to be feared. It is a doorway into another level of existence, a continuation of the soul's infinite voyage. The body may return to the earth, but the essence that animates it, the consciousness, the awareness, the love— lives eternally. Once we truly understand this, our fear of death dissolves, replaced by a quiet reverence for the magnificent cycle of life.

Chapter 15

UFOs: Actual Proof of Their Existence

For over sixty years, our government has continued to lie to us regarding UFOs. It all started with the Roswell incident. The United States government has a secret file on alien activities on our planet that they do not, under any circumstance, want the American people to know about.

Yes, it all began with the Roswell, New Mexico UFO incident on July 8, 1947. The government immediately covered it up by giving the ridiculous story that it was a weather balloon. Very few people know that our government made a secret pact with malevolent aliens in order to obtain their technology.

President Eisenhower was the very first president to come in contact with an alien life form. According to research done by very reputable people, President Eisenhower met with aliens on February 19, 1955, at

Holloman Air Force Base in New Mexico. This was actually his second meeting with extraterrestrials.

Currently, there are thousands of alien ships surrounding our planet. They are purposely flying at high altitudes so people are not aware of them. Here is the actual picture of the 1955 UFO crash that was recently released.

Numerous UFO Sightings and Government Secrecy

Numerous sightings of unidentified flying objects have been reported by dozens of pilots flying across the Pacific Ocean over the last two months, according to UFO researcher Ben Hansen. Hansen is a former FBI federal agent who graduated from the University of Utah with a degree in sociology and criminology. He worked for multiple private and public agencies as a crime scene investigator and has recently applied those same skills to paranormal investigations.

He obtained new footage and air traffic control recordings that reveal baffled pilots struggling to describe their bizarre midair sightings.

Hansen compiled these accounts from pilots working with Southwest Airlines, Hawaiian Airlines, and others. In one particularly captivating account, a former military pilot reported seeing multiple aircraft flying above him.

Another reference I want to direct you to is the research from Dr. Steven Greer. Steven Macon Greer, born in 1955, is an American ufologist and retired physician. He founded the Center for the Study of Extraterrestrial Intelligence (CSETI) and the Disclosure Project, both of which seek the release of alleged classified UFO information. He received his Bachelor of Science degree in biology from Appalachian State University in 1982 and his M.D. degree from the James H. Quillen College of Medicine at East Tennessee State University in 1987. After obtaining his Virginia medical license in 1989, he worked as an emergency room physician before retiring in 1988.

Dr. Greer has gone to Congress several times, urging lawmakers to reveal to the public the truth about our government's involvement with UFOs. However, each time, there was an immediate gag order placed on his request.

Phil Schneider was a U.S. government geologist and engineer involved in the construction of Deep Underground Military Bases, known as DUMBs. He was later assassinated by a U.S. intelligence agency for disclosing information about the government's cover-up of UFOs and aliens. Before his death, he toured across the United States speaking about various subjects, including his role in building a secret underground base in Dulce, New Mexico, for the military. During that time, he reportedly had an encounter with a malevolent extraterrestrial race in the late 1970s that changed his life completely. I actually had the opportunity to attend one of his lectures when he came to Denver.

Next, we have Dr. Linus Pauling, who held a Ph.D. in mathematical physics and physical chemistry from Caltech. Pauling won multiple Nobel Prizes and was listed among the top twenty scientists of all time by New Scientist magazine. He not only believed in UFOs and extraterrestrial life but also conducted research on the subject.

From the research I have done, I have noticed that there are different types of UFO crafts—cigar-shaped, triangular, and saucer-shaped. However, our government continues to deny their existence. It is also tragic that the vast majority of people have been brainwashed into believing the government's lies regarding UFOs.

Here is a picture that I found of a cigar-shaped UFO.

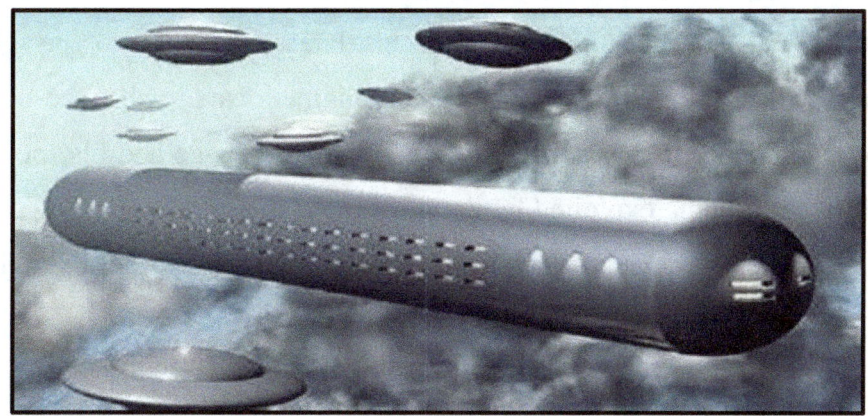

Extraterrestrial Motherships and David Adair

Also there are what are called Mother Ships. The head of the Pentagon's unidentified aerial phenomena research office noted in a report that was recently drafted that there is a possibility that extraterrestrial motherships and smaller probes may be visiting planets in our solar system. A massive alien spacecraft, around the size of the US state of Idaho, has been spotted near the sun by ufologists in recent NASA pictures. They say the object definitely has a structure. Hence, Mother Ships can have a size from just a few miles in diameter to hundreds of miles.

You also need to take a look at the remarkable accomplishments of David Adair. Adair was a child prodigy and is now an internationally recognized expert in space technology and industrial applications. At the age of seventeen, he received the "Most Outstanding in the Field of Engineering Services" award from the U.S. Air Force. He has shared his personal account of being taken to Groom Lake, commonly known as Area 51, as a teenager along with his latest rocket prototype. He described examining a UFO propulsion engine located under the base and explained how he managed to keep his knowledge and his rocket design from being exploited by the military. It is well known that Area 51 has been associated with multiple UFO crash retrievals over the years.

Chapter 16

The Billy Meier Story

Another fascinating and mysterious case that continues to intrigue researchers and truth-seekers alike is that of Billy Eduard Albert Meier, often known simply as Billy Meier. He is an ordinary man by appearance, a one-armed farmer from Switzerland, yet his story stands among the most extraordinary in modern history. Over the course of several decades, Meier has captured hundreds of photographs that he claims are authentic images of extraterrestrial spacecraft—what he refers to as "Beam Ships." He has also recorded videos, audio samples, and detailed transcripts describing his encounters with beings from beyond our planet.

Meier's claims are centered on intelligent entities he calls the Pleiadians, or Plejaren as they identify themselves. These beings, according to his accounts, originate from a star system near the constellation of the Pleiades. They are described as advanced in both technology and consciousness, existing on a spiritual and ethical level far beyond our current human understanding. Meier insists that their purpose is not domination or interference but education, to help humanity awaken to universal laws, self-responsibility, and the need for harmony with nature.

Billy Meier was born in the small Swiss town of Bülach on February 3, 1937. His story began when he was a child. From a very young age, he reportedly experienced telepathic contact with non-human intelligences who would later identify themselves as the Pleiadians. These early encounters shaped the course of his entire life and set the foundation for what would become one of the most documented and controversial contact cases ever recorded.

His first formally recorded meeting took place on January 28, 1975. On that day, Meier claimed to have met a female Pleiadian named Semjase, who would become his primary contact for many years. She was said to be graceful, youthful, and kind, radiating wisdom and a deep sense of peace. Over the years, their relationship evolved into a form of teacher and student dynamic, in which she shared profound knowledge about cosmology, the evolution of consciousness, and the destiny of humankind.

According to Meier, Semjase explained that humanity is still in its infancy in terms of spiritual evolution. The Pleiadians see us as a species capable of great love and creativity but also burdened by ignorance, materialism, and violence. Their mission, she said, was to guide humanity toward a deeper awareness of universal truths—truths about energy, frequency, and the interconnectedness of all living beings.

During several of their encounters, Meier was permitted to photograph her Beam Ship as it performed complex flight maneuvers in the skies above the Swiss countryside. Many of these photographs show metallic, disc-shaped crafts hovering over trees or distant mountains. The clarity and composition of these images have fascinated investigators and skeptics alike. Some of the footage has been analyzed by experts who found no evidence of tampering or miniature models, while others remain unconvinced, suggesting possible fabrication. Yet, despite decades of scrutiny, much of the evidence remains unexplainable.

Beyond the photographs, Meier produced audio recordings of the ship's distinctive humming sound and even physical metal samples said to have been given to him by his extraterrestrial contacts. These materials were reportedly examined by scientists and found to contain unusual isotopic ratios that could not easily be replicated on Earth at the time. Whether one believes in the authenticity of these claims or not, the volume and consistency of his evidence make his case one of the most studied and enduring in UFO research.

Perhaps what makes the Billy Meier story so compelling is not just the physical evidence but the spiritual message that accompanies it. His Pleiadian contacts emphasized the importance of peace, truth, and balance. They warned of humanity's destructive tendencies and the potential collapse of civilization if we continue to exploit the planet and each other. Yet they also spoke of hope—a hope rooted in human potential and the ability to rise above ignorance through understanding and compassion.

In the end, whether one views Meier as a prophet of higher truths or merely a man with an extraordinary imagination, his story continues to spark deep questions about who we are, where we come from, and what lies beyond the boundaries of our world. His experiences challenge the limits of conventional science and invite us to consider the possibility that life, intelligence, and consciousness are far more vast and interconnected than we have ever imagined.

Here is an actual picture of Billy and Semjase.

The Billy Meier Contacts and Their Teachings

Acting as a mediator and spokesperson for the Pleiadians from the planet Erra, Billy Meier shares their profound and esoteric teachings with humanity. Through him, they seek to guide Earth's people back onto the spiritual path we abandoned long ago. Billy has taken over a thousand of the clearest photographs of extraterrestrial spacecraft ever recorded. His conversations with these beings were documented word-for-word and include remarkable insights about Earth's history, humanity, science, and spirituality.

Randolph Winters traveled to Switzerland to meet Billy and spent three weeks interviewing him. He recorded their conversations on cassette tapes. When Winters returned to the United States, I attended one of his lectures in Denver, Colorado, and purchased all ten of his tapes. Since 1989, Billy has continued to have approximately four contacts a year with Ptaah, the father of Semjase, and he has now had more than 250 contacts in total.

Recently, at the National Press Club, the UFO advocacy group Paradigm Research hosted a five-day event modeled after congressional hearings. They paid former senators and representatives, including Mike Gravel, Roscoe Bartlett, Merrill Cook, Lynn Woolsey, Carolyn Kilpatrick, and Darlene Hooley, to review evidence of UFO sightings and the possibility of advanced extraterrestrial life. The goal was to encourage the government to disclose what it knows about UFOs. To say that conspiracy theories surrounded the event would be an understatement, but the testimonies presented were powerful.

The panel heard from Peter Davenport, director of the National UFO Reporting Center, who shared eyewitness accounts of UFOs hovering motionless in the sky and changing direction in ways that defy known technology. He recounted sightings from McMinnville, Tennessee, in 1995, where witnesses observed hovering lights that appeared to explode, and from Phoenix in 1997, where residents saw an enormous craft silently moving over the city. In 1999, two airline pilots near Dallas–Fort Worth reported seeing a large disc make a 120-degree turn in under a second. "I have no explanation for a craft that can hover motionless above Phoenix for five minutes," Davenport told the panel.

Peter Robbins, a researcher and lecturer, spoke about incidents like the famous Rendlesham Forest sighting in the United Kingdom, where U.S. Air Force personnel witnessed an unidentified object. Gary Heseltine, a former U.K. police detective, shared data from over 425 cases involving more than 940 British police officers, most of which had multiple witnesses.

Journalist Linda Moulton Howe, known for her investigations into livestock mutilations, presented slides of cattle and horses that had been surgically dissected with precision and left bloodless. Ranchers had reportedly seen glowing discs shining beams of light onto their animals and even lifting them into the air. One photograph showed a cow with its udder cleanly removed and no trace of blood, while another revealed serrated incisions made with what veterinarians said must have been high-heat instruments. "I think it involves, on a more sophisticated level, what we are beginning to do in our science with cloning," Howe explained when asked by former Rep. Lynn Woolsey what extraterrestrials might want with cow parts. "The agencies of the U.S. government, the CIA—they have all been studying this. They have more data than I do."

I have personally researched the UFO phenomenon for more than I have personally researched the UFO phenomenon for more than twenty-five years. Our government has been deceiving us for over six decades about its involvement with extraterrestrial entities. People need to understand that there are three main types of ETs. Some have a negative agenda and have performed harmful experiments on humans against their will. Others are neutral observers who monitor events on our planet. The third group, the benevolent ETs, have come to assist us. Their mission is to help humanity understand its higher purpose and to raise our collective consciousness to make this world a better place. I believe these benevolent beings are now in full control.

Many people remain fearful of alien contact, but that fear is unnecessary. The benevolent ETs intend to reveal themselves in an open and peaceful way in the near future. They will only do so when humanity is ready and capable of accepting their presence without panic or hostility.

I have said before and I will say again—there are thousands of alien ships orbiting Earth right now. They remain at high altitudes so as not to alarm the general public. In just the past few months, dozens of pilots flying over the Pacific Ocean have reported sightings of unidentified craft. How much more evidence do people need before they awaken to the truth? We have been lied to and conditioned to deny what is right before our eyes.

Chapter 17

Astral Projection

Astral projection is the remarkable concept that a person can consciously separate their awareness from the physical body and travel through what is known as the astral plane. This journey is undertaken through a subtle form of energy called the astral body, which mirrors the physical form yet exists on a higher vibrational level. Throughout history, this phenomenon has been described under many names, including astral travel, soul journey, spiritual wandering, and out-of-body exploration. The word "astral" itself means "of the stars," suggesting that this plane of existence is vast, luminous, and interwoven with the very fabric of the cosmos. The astral body is believed to reside between the mental and spiritual dimensions of being, acting as a bridge between thought and divine awareness.

People who have experienced astral projection often speak of a moment of transition that feels both liberating and deeply peaceful.

They describe sensations of floating, spinning, or rolling gently out of their physical form. Some report feeling a light vibration throughout their body just before separation, while others sense a distinct "pulling" or "lifting" motion as their consciousness shifts. Once free, many find themselves hovering near their sleeping body, observing it from above before exploring the environment around them. The experience is often accompanied by a profound sense of freedom, clarity, and connection to something much greater than themselves.

Those who travel through the astral plane describe it as a realm filled with fluidity and limitless possibility. Physical laws such as gravity and time seem to lose their grip. In this space, thought itself becomes the vehicle of movement. You can glide effortlessly through walls, fly above landscapes, or appear instantly at a distant location simply by focusing your intention. Some explorers recount visiting breathtaking places filled with radiant light, color, and harmony, while others encounter symbolic representations of their inner world, places that mirror their emotions, memories, and spiritual state.

Astral projection can occur spontaneously, often during moments of deep relaxation, meditation, or sleep paralysis. However, when practiced intentionally, it becomes a conscious and controlled process. Unlike the frightening paralysis that can sometimes accompany unintentional out-of-body states, true astral projection is generally peaceful. The practitioner remains calm, aware, and in control. The key lies in maintaining a delicate balance between wakefulness and surrender, between conscious thought and effortless letting go.

One of the most respected institutions in the world dedicated to studying this phenomenon is the Monroe Institute, located in the United States. For more than half a century, this organization has been a pioneering center for the scientific and experiential exploration of consciousness. Founded by Robert Monroe, a man whose own spontaneous out-of-body experiences led him to decades of research, the institute continues to help individuals access expanded states of awareness beyond the confines of the physical body.

The Monroe Institute offers a range of immersive programs designed to help participants safely explore these states through guided techniques and audio frequencies that synchronize the brain's hemispheres. Among their most fascinating offerings is an online program called Bilocation, which is available through their website at monroeinstitute.org/products. This course teaches individuals how to experience being in two places at once, a concept that once belonged solely to mystics and spiritual masters. Through focused mental exercises and relaxation methods, participants learn to shift their consciousness from one location to another while still maintaining awareness of their physical surroundings. It is said that with practice, the boundary between physical and non-physical experience begins to dissolve, revealing the extraordinary nature of human consciousness.

Many who have studied at the Monroe Institute report transformative experiences, describing a newfound sense of unity and freedom. They often return with a deeper understanding that consciousness is not confined to the brain or the body, but rather a vast, timeless field of awareness that can exist independently of the physical world. Astral projection, therefore, is not merely a curiosity or a mystical pursuit. It is a reminder of who we truly are, spiritual beings having a temporary human experience, capable of exploring dimensions far beyond the limits of the material realm.

Chapter 18

Government Lies and Secret Programs

Understanding government secrecy gives you power—the power to resist manipulation and to see beyond the illusions that shape our world. I have been privileged to meet people who worked within government intelligence circles, including former CIA and FBI agents and whistleblowers. Through them, I have learned things the public was never meant to know.

Wearing a Mask: Was It a Con?

This next subject is politically charged, but I encourage everyone to approach it with an open mind and to verify the facts for themselves. Oxygen is vital for every cell in our body. When oxygen levels decrease, it can lead to chronic fatigue, poor concentration, low energy, headaches, stress, reduced libido, and even heart disease.

The reason I raise this issue is that prolonged mask-wearing significantly reduces the oxygen available to our cells. Despite what we were told, masks may not have been as safe or effective as claimed. Researchers like epidemiologist Boris Borovoy and scientists Colleen Huber and Q. Makeeta have warned about the dangers of inhaling microplastics and nanoplastics from disposable masks. Even opening a new package can release these particles. With prolonged use, the risk of inhaling them increases, allowing them to enter the lungs and potentially cause harm.

A recent study published in Cancer Discovery found that long-term inhalation of harmful microbes and materials could contribute to advanced stages of lung cancer. Extended mask use can also encourage the growth of dangerous pathogens. This evidence should concern any physician or epidemiologist who understands occupational health risks. I urge everyone to look at the research themselves rather than relying solely on what they were told.

Epidemiologist Boris Borovoy, along with researchers Colleen Huber and Q. Makeeta, were among the first to warn about the dangers of inhaling microplastics and nanoplastics from disposable surgical masks. They explained that this risk begins the moment the masks are removed from their packaging, as fibers can detach and enter the lungs. The longer a mask is worn, the more fibers are released into the air.

Their concern was clear: if widespread mask use continued, hundreds of millions of people could be inhaling foreign materials daily, creating serious long-term health risks. This warning, they said, should alarm every physician and epidemiologist familiar with occupational hazards.

A study published in Cancer Discovery further suggested that inhaling harmful microbes trapped within masks might contribute to the development of advanced lung cancer over time. Microbiologists added that frequent mask use creates a moist environment where bacteria and fungi can thrive. Once inhaled, these microbes can travel through the trachea and bronchi into the delicate alveoli of the lungs, where they may cause lasting damage. Yet, information like this has been repeatedly dismissed or censored.

One of the most debated reports came from a study associated with Stanford University, which appeared briefly on the National Center for Biotechnology Information website. It claimed that face masks were ineffective against COVID-19 transmission, stating that the SARS-CoV-2 virus, measuring between 60 and 140 nanometers, could easily pass through mask fibers that are over a thousand times larger. Although the study was later removed, its contents fueled further skepticism about official narratives surrounding masks.

The World Health Organization's own early statements acknowledged the lack of direct evidence supporting universal masking for healthy individuals, noting that no conclusive studies existed on preventing infection through mask use. However, that guidance was quickly replaced, and much of the original language vanished from public view.

Researchers and medical experts who opposed mask mandates also argued that prolonged use reduces oxygen intake and increases carbon dioxide rebreathing. Elevated CO_2 levels can lead to hypercapnia, a condition marked by confusion, rapid heart rate, and fatigue. Chronic oxygen deprivation, known as hypoxia, can cause headaches, chest pain, and even organ damage if left untreated.

An OSHA expert with two decades of experience in workplace safety claimed that mask use could lower oxygen levels to as little as 17 percent within minutes, far below the agency's safe minimum of 19.5 percent. This, too, was met with immediate censorship.

Neurosurgeon Dr. Russell Blaylock expressed similar concerns, stating that prolonged mask use could cause airway resistance, carbon dioxide buildup, and potentially life-threatening complications. He also warned that trapped viruses could accumulate in nasal passages and travel through the olfactory nerves to the brain.

Critics argue that government agencies downplayed or concealed these findings to serve powerful corporate interests. They suggest that the mask industry and pharmaceutical companies benefited from widespread public fear and compliance, prioritizing profit over health. Censorship, they claim, has become a tool to maintain control of public opinion and suppress dissent.

As former CIA Director William Casey once said, "We'll know our disinformation program is complete when everything the American public believes is false."

Chapter 19

Danger of Vaccines

This section is controversial. At first, I wasn't going to include it, but it would be a disservice not to mention it. The question that continues to divide experts and parents alike is this: Do vaccines in children cause autism?

If you search the topic online, nearly every result will claim that vaccines do not cause autism. Yet one must ask, is that truly the case, or just another carefully constructed deception? After reviewing the evidence presented here, you must decide for yourself.

Dr. William Thompson, a senior scientist at the Centers for Disease Control and Prevention, came forward as a whistleblower, claiming that he and his superiors were instructed to destroy data linking vaccines to autism. Soon after, a group of more than a dozen CDC scientists sent a letter to the agency's Chief of Staff, Carmen Villar, expressing serious concerns about internal corruption and unethical conduct. They objected to intimidation, data manipulation, and the influence of external parties that distorted the agency's policies. Their warnings were quickly buried.

From my research, there appears to be a correlation between the age at which a child is vaccinated and the likelihood of developing autism. It is medically known that a newborn has a weak or undeveloped immune system. Full immune function does not mature until around the age of six. Administering multiple vaccines before that point places immense stress on a child's developing body. Yet the FDA continues to push vaccination from infancy, a decision that many believe serves corporate profit rather than public health.

A CDC study reported that infants exposed to only sixty-three micrograms of mercury were two and a half times more likely to develop autism. Most babies, however, receive numerous injections containing up to two hundred micrograms or more before reaching two years of age—significantly compounding the risk. Despite this, the government and vaccine manufacturers continue to deny any connection between vaccines and autism.

Every vaccine contains adjuvants, chemical compounds designed to enhance immune response but often toxic to the human body. These substances include phenol, formaldehyde, acetone, aluminum, glycerin, MSG, and mercury in the form of thimerosal. Thimerosal, once banned in over-the-counter medications in 1998, remains present in many vaccines and is the third most toxic substance known to medical science.

Over time, these ingredients have been linked to ADHD, asthma, learning disabilities, diabetes, and neurological disorders.

Some researchers go further, suggesting that these formulations are not merely dangerous but intentionally designed to impair and control future generations. The American Health Service in Michigan has warned that vaccines may contain compounds capable of altering neurological development and behavior. Meanwhile, over 250 new vaccines are currently in development, raising questions about the motives driving their expansion. It is also worth noting that U.S. law grants vaccine manufacturers complete legal immunity, preventing citizens from suing them for vaccine-related injury or death.

The FDA's own Vaccine Adverse Event Reporting System (VAERS) receives approximately eleven thousand reports of serious vaccine reactions each year, though independent analysts estimate the true number may exceed one hundred thousand annually. Many cases go unreported due to institutional pressure on physicians. Studies have also connected vaccines with sudden infant death syndrome (SIDS), suggesting that these tragedies may not be as "unexplained" as once thought.

The same lack of transparency appears in the reporting of COVID-19 deaths. In an interview conducted by Tony Robbins, several physicians claimed that over eighty percent of deaths attributed to COVID-19 occurred among elderly patients with serious preexisting conditions. They accused public health agencies of manipulating statistics to sustain fear and compliance.

A document released by the American Medical Association reportedly trained doctors to use misleading terminology when discussing pandemic data. On page nine, it advised physicians to equate hospitalizations with deaths in order to heighten public concern. Elsewhere, the same guide suggested replacing the word "lockdown" with "stay-at-home order" to soften its authoritarian implications. Physicians were instructed to deflect questions about vaccine injury and maintain a uniform narrative, prioritizing message control over open dialogue.

According to critics, this approach turns doctors into public relations agents rather than healers. Real medicine has taken a back seat to politics, profit, and control.

The debate over the COVID-19 vaccine further highlights this division. According to the American Heritage College Dictionary, a vaccine is "a preparation of a weakened pathogen that stimulates antibody production but is incapable of causing severe infection." The CDC quietly altered this definition to classify COVID-19 injections as vaccines, despite their inability to prevent infection or transmission. They also labeled them "experimental," underscoring the uncertainty surrounding their long-term effects.

The emergence of Long COVID—a condition marked by chronic fatigue, neurological issues, and respiratory distress—has raised further questions. No other vaccine in history has required a "long" classification, and the medical community still struggles to define or treat it effectively

One example of medical suppression involves Dr. Richard, a practitioner who successfully treated patients with herbal remedies for cancer and other serious diseases. His success drew the ire of pharmaceutical interests. In a dramatic raid, agents from the FDA and AMA confiscated his equipment, shut down his clinic, and had him arrested. Though he was eventually released, his persecution sent a clear message: natural cures threaten profit, and profit cannot be threatened.

Nature has already provided humanity with every cure it needs. Plants, herbs, and natural compounds offer treatments for countless illnesses, including cancer. Yet the medical establishment, driven by greed, works to obscure these truths and maintain dependency on synthetic pharmaceuticals.

Consider the words of several physicians who spoke out long before COVID-19:

"Only after realizing that routine immunizations were dangerous did I achieve a substantial drop in infant death rates. The worst vaccine of all is the whooping cough vaccine. It is responsible for many deaths and irreversible brain damage." — Dr. Kalokerinos, M.D.

"If we look closely, we realize that 'health for all,' according to the WHO, means drugs and vaccinations for all. That is to say, sickness for all." — Dr. Guylaine Lanctot, M.D.

"I've been practicing for forty years, and in the past twenty, children have been sicker than ever." — Dr. Doris J. Rapp.

"This report describes six mothers who received live virus vaccines and one who received a hepatitis B vaccine during pregnancy, after having received an MMR booster five months prior to conception. All seven children had developmental problems; six were diagnosed with autism, and the seventh with an autism spectrum disorder." — Dr. F. Edward Yazbak, M.D.

"Public policy regarding vaccines is fundamentally flawed. It is permeated by conflicts of interest, based on inadequate studies insulated from independent scrutiny. The evidence is far too poor to justify overriding the independent judgments of patients, parents, and physicians." — Association of American Physicians.

"There is no evidence that any influenza vaccine thus far developed is effective. The producers of these vaccines know they are worthless but continue selling them anyway. There is, however, much evidence proving that immunization of children does more harm than good." — Dr. J. Anthony Morris, former FDA Vaccine Control Officer.

Even outside the U.S., skepticism toward the FDA is widespread. In Mexico, healthcare professionals often refer to it as the Federal Death Administration—a grim nickname that reflects a growing global mistrust of American health policy.

Chapter 20

Global Depopulation Agenda

I came across an interview with Mike Yeadon, a thirty-two-year veteran of the pharmaceutical industry who once served as Vice President of Allergy and Respiratory Research at Pfizer. A microbiologist and expert on viral respiratory infections, Yeadon shared a chilling and deeply unsettling perspective during an interview conducted before the outbreak of COVID-19. His words have since echoed through countless discussions about global health, power, and control.

He said, "If you wanted to depopulate a significant portion of the world and to do it in a way that wouldn't destroy the environment with nuclear weapons or poison everyone with anthrax, and you wanted plausible deniability while maintaining a multi-year infectious disease crisis, I don't think you could come up with a better plan than what we are seeing unfold before us."

Yeadon's statement was more than speculative—it carried the weight of someone who had spent decades inside the very system he was describing. He went on to explain, "The eugenicists have taken control of the levers of power. This is an artful way of getting people to line up and receive something that will damage them. It will not kill them immediately, because that would be obvious. Instead, it will produce gradual, normal pathology—something that can be blamed on other causes over time."

Then he added, almost as if to conclude the thought: "That's what I would do if I wanted to eliminate ninety to ninety-five percent of the world's population. And I think that's exactly what they're doing." His words were chilling not only because of their content, but because they came from someone who knew the mechanisms of the pharmaceutical world from within.

This concept—that depopulation might be masked as public health or environmental necessity—is not new. It has been echoed, sometimes bluntly, by influential figures across academia, government, and industry for decades.

Dr. Eric Pianka from the University of Texas once compared population growth to cancer, saying, "A cancer is an uncontrolled multiplication of cells. The population explosion is an uncontrolled multiplication of people. We must shift from treating the symptoms to cutting out the cancer. The operation will require many brutal and heartless decisions." His words, though metaphorical, reveal a mindset in which human life becomes a statistical burden, something to be "managed" rather than valued.

Stanford professor Paul Ehrlich echoed similar sentiments, stating, "We have to take away from humans their reproductive autonomy in the long run as the only way to guarantee the advancement of mankind." Such a statement, under the banner of scientific progress, raises difficult moral and ethical questions about who gets to decide the fate of others in the name of humanity's "advancement."

Even Francis Crick, the discoverer of the DNA double-helix structure, weighed in on the topic. He once remarked, "There is a single theme behind all our work: we must reduce population levels. Either governments do it through clean methods, or we will see the chaos we've witnessed in El Salvador, Iran, or Beirut. Once population is out of control, it takes authoritarian government—even fascism—to bring it down. To reduce the population quickly, you must send men to war and eliminate a significant number of fertile women. The fastest ways to do that are famine and disease." Crick's words show a cold rationalism—a utilitarian logic stripped of empathy—that has appeared repeatedly in elite discussions about global population management.

Thomas Ferguson, from the U.S. State Department's Office of Population Affairs, stated, "Depopulation should be the highest priority of foreign policy toward the third world, because the U.S. economy will require large and increasing amounts of minerals from abroad, especially from less developed countries." This statement revealed the geopolitical layer beneath the surface—a recognition that fewer people in resource-rich nations means easier control and access to their assets.

Dr. Henry Kissinger made similar statements, claiming, "The world's population needs to be reduced by fifty percent," and referring to the elderly as "useless eaters." He also warned, "It is easier to kill a million people than to control a million people. People are fighting back, and our capacity to impose control over humanity is at a historical low." Kissinger's perspective hinted at both frustration and strategy—a belief that maintaining control over billions is harder than simply reducing their numbers.

Zbigniew Brzezinski, political scientist and former National Security Advisor to Presidents Johnson and Carter, expressed similar ideas when he stated, "The vast overpopulation far beyond the world's carrying capacity cannot be solved by future reductions in birth rates. It must be met now by reducing existing numbers by whatever means necessary." His statement exposes the same theme: that the problem of "too many people" justifies nearly any means to correct it.

Ted Turner, founder of CNN and major United Nations contributor, summed it up with striking bluntness: "A total population of 250 to 300 million people, a 95 percent decline, would be ideal." When someone of his influence expresses such views so openly, it forces one to question how deeply such thinking has seeped into global institutions and policies.

In 1992, thirty-two world governments signed the Rio de Janeiro Treaty, which, according to reports, included provisions aligning with global depopulation goals. Figures such as Bill Gates, Anthony Fauci, and Klaus Schwab have all been accused of supporting this agenda, alongside agencies like the WHO and the UN. Whether one believes these claims or not, the sheer level of coordination, funding, and policy alignment between global powers raises troubling questions about intent, transparency, and accountability.

It's evident that discussions of population reduction long predate the COVID-19 pandemic. The language of "sustainability" and "climate resilience" often overlaps eerily with older depopulation rhetoric. Yet if you search the term "depopulation agenda" today, you'll find it dismissed almost universally as nothing more than a conspiracy theory. Go figure.

Chapter 21

Project MK-Ultra: The Government's Program to Control Your Mind

It has become clear to me that most Americans are living under a form of psychological control engineered by their own government— yet remain unaware that their thoughts and emotions are being manipulated. The origins of this program trace back to **Project Paperclip**, under which Nazi SS scientists were brought to the United States after World War II. These scientists laid the groundwork for what would later become known as **Project MK-Ultra**—the government's secret mind-control initiative.

Over seventy years later, the program has evolved into something far more advanced. With the rise of artificial intelligence, surveillance networks, and neural technologies, mind control has become not just possible but increasingly sophisticated. Such programs thrive in a climate of fear, secrecy, conformity, and blind trust—fueled by unlimited government funding.

Albert Einstein once said, *"Blind belief in authority is the greatest enemy of truth."* That truth is more relevant today than ever.

In the early 1970s, hundreds of inmates at the Gunnison Facility in Utah were reportedly subjected to experiments involving **scalar wave technology**—a form of energy capable of influencing brain function.

81

These experiments aimed to implant thoughts, induce voices, and manipulate emotions remotely. The University of Utah led much of the research at the time, exploring how scalar waves could be used to override the human mind.

In 1988, a man named David Fratus, imprisoned at Utah's Draper facility, claimed he began hearing voices as clearly as though he were wearing stereo headphones. He believed the voices were being transmitted through scalar beams linked to satellites, HAARP transmitters, and a network of GWEN towers located approximately every two hundred miles across the United States. The messages, he said, were identical to those heard by other prisoners—messages said to be of "alien origin."

Dr. Eldon Byrd, a U.S. Naval officer and scalar technology researcher, presented his findings at the 2000 U.S. Psychotronics Association Conference. He stated, "Is mind control possible? Absolutely. There is a mountain of evidence. Today we know there are technologies that can induce sound into the brain at a distance, alter brainwaves and behavior remotely, create pain anywhere in the body, and even project images into the mind. Mind control technology exists—without question."

Modern satellite and scalar systems have made it possible to influence entire populations simultaneously. Governments can, in theory, manipulate mood, decision-making, and even social unrest through electromagnetic and frequency-based methods.

Adding to this is what some call the "***Dumbing Down of Humanity***" initiative. With the constant use of mobile devices, people have stopped retaining knowledge and critical thought, relying instead on external inputs. This makes it easier to direct thought patterns and shape perception.

Your mind is your most precious asset. It must be protected. Simply recognizing that manipulation exists is the first step toward resistance. You can retrain your subconscious to reject negative programming by maintaining awareness and critical thought.

One of the most powerful defenses against mind control is to raise your frequency—emotionally, mentally, and spiritually. Fear is the lowest frequency and keeps people trapped. Love is the highest and most effective shield. Surround yourself with it, cultivate it, and extend it to others.

There are countless resources online that offer techniques for self-protection and mental sovereignty. Simply search *"how to protect yourself from mind control."* Knowledge, awareness, and love remain our greatest weapons.

Chapter 22

CIA Project Pandora Microwave Remote Brain Manipulation

Dr Ross Adey's research at the Brain Research Institute of the University of California was funded by the CIA. In their Pandora project, a catalog of different brain signals for specific actions, emotions and pathological states of mind was recorded. It was found that when microwaves were used to fire these signals at victims' brains, they experienced the moods, behavior, and pathological states, carried by the signals. This meant that by mimicking natural brain frequencies, the human brain could be controlled remotely by use of extremely low-frequency broadcast carried by pulse-modulated microwave beams (ELF pulse-modulated microwave remote mind control technology). For more info, you can Google Microwave Mind Control by Tim Rifat. Intelligence operatives can induce remote conditioning by creating information-processing effects that can cause excitatory reactions, subliminal stress, behavioral arousal, enhanced suggestibility by inhibition of higher functions, and patterned behaviors. It is alleged that this technology is used by the CIA and MI5 to modify the behavior of 'high-profile subversives.

The more advanced electronic Remote Mind-Control Technology (RMCT) utilizes ELF-modulated lasers for long-range, penetrative, invasive EM mind control. Together with Doppler-shifted interrogative RMCT masers, a victim's brain-states can be analyzed at a distance-and the 'subversive' can be modified at a distance. Developments in this technique, and the use of low-frequency EM radiation to see through walls, have allowed intelligence agencies in the US to make useful inroads on the path to synthetic telepathy. Much of this research has been funded by the CIA which began this work on electronic mind control with its Pandora project. This research was used to build devices like RHIC-EDOM (Radio Hypnotic Intracerebral Control – Electronic Dissolution of Memory), which is allegedly used for forced induction of hypnotic trance in the abduction of and experimentation upon civilians by US Government agencies.

Chapter 23

The Nuremberg Trials and Accord and How it Relates to Vaccines

The Nuremberg trials first began on November 20, 1945, with 24 high-ranking Nazi officials facing charges including war crimes, crimes against peace, and crimes against humanity. Conducted by the International Military Tribunal, composed of judges from the United States, Great Britain, France, and the Soviet Union, the trials aimed to hold individuals accountable for their actions and set a precedent for international law. The authority of the International Military Tribunal to conduct these trials stemmed from the London Agreement of August 8, 1945.

On that date, representatives from the United States, Great Britain, the Soviet Union, and the provisional government of France signed an agreement that included a charter for an international military tribunal to conduct trials of major Axis war criminals whose offenses had no particular geographic location. Later, 19 other nations accepted the provisions of this agreement. The tribunal was given the authority to find any individual guilty of the commission of war crimes and to declare any group or organization to be criminal in character. The Nuremberg Accord also outlines laws governing medical establishments. According to the Nuremberg Code #1, all medical procedures have to have voluntary consent. Here is a summary of what the Code exactly what this code states.

The voluntary consent of the human subject is absolutely essential. This means that the person involved should have legal capacity to give consent; should be situated as to be able to exercise free power of choice, without the intervention of any element of force, fraud, deceit, duress, over-reaching, or other ulterior form of constraint or coercion, and should have sufficient knowledge and comprehension of the elements of the subject matter involved as to enable him to make an understanding and enlightened decision.

This latter element requires that before the acceptance of an affirmative decision by the experimental subject there should be made known to him the nature, duration, and purpose of the experiment; the method and means by which it is to be conducted; all inconveniences and hazards reasonably to be expected; and the effects upon his health or person which may possibly come from his participation in the experiment.

The duty and responsibility for ascertaining the quality of the consent rests upon each individual who initiates, directs or engages in the experiment. It is a personal duty and responsibility which may not be delegated to another with impunity. Sometime during the year 2021 a team of over 1,000 lawyers and over 10,000 medical experts led by Dr. Reiner Fuellmich began legal proceedings against the CDC, WHO & the Davos Group for crimes against humanity. Doctors use a test called a PCR test. A medical PCR (polymerase chain reaction) test is a laboratory technique that amplifies tiny amounts of genetic material (DNA or RNA) to detect and diagnose a wide range of conditions, from infectious diseases to genetic disorders. However, Fuellmich and his team found the PCR test to be faulty and unreliable. This in turn enabled doctors to classify all deaths as Covid deaths even though the majority of patients had pre-existing conditions.

The *"experimental" COVID vaccine is in violation of all 10 of the Nuremberg Codes which carry the death penalty for those who seek to violate these International Laws. The "vaccine" fails to meet the five requirements to be considered a vaccine and is by definition, a medical "experiment."* The "vaccine" fails to meet the five requirements to be considered a vaccine and is by definition, a medical "experiment."

In addition to the flawed tests and fraudulent death certificates, the "experimental" vaccine itself is in violation of Article 32 of the Geneva Convention. Under Article 32 of the 1949 Geneva Convention. Remember, our U.S. government admitted the COVID-19 vaccine was experimental.

The point of presenting this information to you is so that if you were forced to take the vaccine you have the right, backed by international law, to sue the parties for violating your free will rights.

Chapter 24

Smart Meters – How Safe Are They?

Smart Meters have been associated with privacy, data security, and health concerns arising from radio frequency (RF) radiation. These devices transmit data wirelessly to utility companies, continuously emitting low-level RF radiation. While this technology enhances data collection efficiency, it also exposes residents to uninterrupted electromagnetic emissions and increases vulnerability to invasive data monitoring — not only of household devices but also of daily electrical usage patterns.

In 2011, the World Health Organization classified radiation from Smart Meters as a Class 2-B carcinogen, indicating potential links to cancer. The Karolinska Institute, which awards the Nobel Prizes, subsequently issued a global health warning against wireless Smart Meters, and the American Academy of Environmental Medicine called for a moratorium on their installation. Importantly, Smart Meters never shut off, meaning exposure is ongoing.

Health Implications of RF Exposure

Scientific studies on RF radiation exposure suggest several potential health risks. Prolonged exposure to Smart Meter radiation has been associated with:

- Sleep disturbances due to disrupted melatonin production, which directly affects sleep quality.
- Headaches and fatigue, often attributed to nervous system irritation from electromagnetic exposure.
- Cellular stress, where constant low-level radiation increases oxidative stress, potentially leading to long-term health complications.
- Neurological symptoms, such as brain fog, memory lapses, and difficulty concentrating, linked to heightened electromagnetic fields (EMFs).

Additional reports associate Smart Meter radiation with irritability, nausea, flu-like symptoms, DNA damage, and numerous other ailments. Moreover, there is growing concern regarding a connection between RF radiation and the decline of honeybee populations and other animal species.

Radiation and Environmental Exposure

Unlike traditional analogue meters, Smart Meters emit radiofrequency (RF) radiation in regular, rhythmic pulses, contributing to the cumulative electromagnetic field (EMF) levels within their immediate surroundings. Unlike the continuous and relatively low background radiation from natural sources, these sharp bursts of RF energy occur thousands of times per day, creating a persistent layer of artificial frequency interference. The placement of these devices further increases potential risk. They are often mounted on exterior walls adjacent to bedrooms, living areas, or home offices—spaces where people spend significant time in close proximity. This constant nearness can result in long-term, low-level exposure that compounds over time. 89 Moreover, RF signals are capable of penetrating walls, ceilings, and floors, meaning that even residents who do not have a Smart Meter installed directly on their property may still be affected by the emissions of nearby units. In apartment complexes or densely populated neighborhoods, this overlap of signals can significantly amplify overall indoor exposure levels, creating an invisible but measurable form of environmental pollution.

Data Security and Privacy Risks

Beyond health concerns, Smart Meters pose serious **data privacy vulnerabilities**. By analyzing household energy usage, unauthorized individuals or entities could deduce residents' daily routines — when occupants are home, which appliances are in use, and even specific activities within the home. Intercepting the wireless signals transmitted between the Smart Meter and utility companies could allow for the reconstruction of detailed household behavior profiles.

If such data were accessed through **specialized hardware** such as **software-defined radios (SDRs),** attackers could decode and interpret these signals. This capability could be exploited to determine when homes are unoccupied, increasing the risk of criminal activity. These threats highlight the critical need for **strong encryption, advanced security protocols, and consumer awareness** in Smart Meter implementation.

Minimizing Exposure and Protective Measures

For individuals concerned about EMF exposure, several targeted protective solutions are available:

1. **Smart Meter Shielding Kit** – A specialized EMF shield that blocks RF signals while allowing the meter to function properly.

2. **EMF Shielding Paint** – Applied to walls near the Smart Meter to reduce radiation penetration; can be combined with other EMF barriers for stronger protection.

3. **EMF Shielding Fabric** – Installed behind walls or over windows to prevent radiation from entering living areas.

4. **EMF Canopies** – Suitable for bedrooms adjacent to Smart Meters, these create a low-EMF sleep environment.

5. **EMF Meters** – Tools such as the Tri-Field EMF Meter allow residents to monitor exposure levels and verify the effectiveness of shielding measures.

These solutions, available from reputable EMF safety retailers, help mitigate risks while maintaining utility functionality.

Chapter 25

Directed Energy Weapons Are Real and Disruptive

A **Directed-Energy Weapon (DEW)** is a type of ranged weapon that delivers highly focused energy — such as **lasers, microwaves, particle beams, or sound waves** — to damage or disable a target without using physical projectiles. The U.S. Navy and other branches of the military employ DEWs for power projection and defensive operations due to their precision, controllable effects, and ability to inflict measurable damage at the speed of light.

Understanding DEWs and Their Capabilities

According to the Department of Defense's Joint Publication 313: Electronic Warfare, DEWs represent technologies that produce concentrated electromagnetic energy or subatomic particles. Their applications include:

- Disabling or destroying adversary equipment, facilities, or personnel.
- Disrupting or exploiting the electromagnetic spectrum (EMS) to reduce hostile capabilities.
- Neutralizing enemy electronics, such as drones or communication systems, without kinetic engagement.

As explained by Lieutenant General Henry "Trey" Obering III, USAF (Ret.), former Director of the Missile Defense Agency and Executive Vice President at Booz Allen Hamilton, DEWs are measured 92 by their ability to reliably deliver focused energy that results in precise, repeatable, and controlled damage. Modern DEWs can cut through steel or aluminum within seconds, underscoring their destructive potential.

The Wildfire Question

In recent years, the United States has witnessed an alarming series of catastrophic wildfires.

- In **2018**, the **Paradise, California**, wildfire destroyed the entire town.
- On **December 30, 2021**, the **Marshall Fire** in Colorado erupted, causing mass evacuation and widespread destruction, with no criminal negligence or arson identified.
- On **August 8, 2023**, wildfires devastated **Maui, Hawaii**, resulting in 102 deaths and the destruction of Lahaina — a site of deep historical significance.

- Most recently, on **January 7, 2025, three massive wildfires** broke out almost simultaneously across **Southern California**, prompting the evacuation of over 30,000 residents.

Each of these fires was officially attributed to power company failures, yet the synchronization and intensity of these events have raised serious questions. What are the odds that such massive fires could ignite under near-identical conditions, repeatedly, across different regions?

Investigating Possible Causes

Independent researchers and alternative news outlets have explored the theory that **Directed-Energy Weapon**s may have been involved in triggering these fires. Photographs of the aftermath reveal **patterns inconsistent with typical wildfire behavior** — for example, trees left standing while steel structures were reportedly disintegrated. Naturally occurring fires rarely reach temperatures high enough to vaporize metal, which has fueled speculation that **high-energy beams** may have played a role.

While conclusive evidence remains debated, these unusual characteristics have prompted public scrutiny. Citizens are encouraged to question official narratives and consider the broader implications of advanced technologies possibly being used in ways that remain undisclosed to the public.

The Broader Implications

Never in U.S. history have wildfires occurred at this magnitude and frequency. Whether through deliberate action or systemic negligence, such events contribute to widespread social, emotional, and environmental distress. The possibility that these disasters could be linked to directed-energy systems raises urgent ethical and accountability concerns.

Citizens must remain vigilant, question new incidents critically, and demand transparency from institutions responsible for both **public safety and technological oversight.**

Chapter 26

Propaganda by the News Media -The True Nature of the Media

The most effective form of propaganda succeeds when people believe the information originates from an **authoritative and trustworthy source**. This illusion of credibility is at the core of modern media influence. In truth, many so-called authoritative figures — often tied to government or corporate interests — are paid to promote selective narratives. By positioning these individuals as "experts" or "official voices," the public is conditioned to accept information without question.

This manipulation is tragic but intentional. One of the enduring directives of the U.S. government has been to **indoctrinate the public into accepting distorted truths**. Fake news and misinformation are not new phenomena; they have long been embedded within the framework of American democracy.

The Historical Roots of Media Deception

As far back as the 18th century, prominent leaders expressed deep mistrust of the press. Consider the words of **President Thomas Jefferson**, the principal author of the U.S. Constitution:

"Nothing can now be believed which is seen in a newspaper. Truth itself becomes suspicious by being put into that polluted vehicle. The real extent of this state of misinformation is known only to those who are in situations to confront facts within their knowledge with the lies of the day. The press is impotent when it abandons itself to falsehood."

Jefferson also warned of the inevitable **corruption of power**, stating:

"Experience hath shown that even under the best forms of government those entrusted with power have, in time, and by slow operations, perverted it into tyranny."

These warnings from centuries ago remain startlingly relevant today.

Warnings from History: The Cost of Secrecy

Another U.S. president, **John F. Kennedy**, spoke candidly about the dangers of secrecy and manipulation within power structures:

"The very word 'secrecy' is repugnant in a free and open society; and we are as a people inherently and historically opposed to secret societies, to secret oaths and to secret proceedings... Our way of life is under attack... no war ever posed a greater threat to our security. We are opposed around the world by a monolithic and ruthless conspiracy that relies primarily on covert means for expanding its sphere of influence — infiltration instead of invasion, subversion instead of elections, intimidation instead of free choice... It is a system that has conscripted vast human and material resources into the building of a tightly knit, highly efficient machine... Its mistakes are buried, not 96 headlined. Its dissenters are silenced, not praised. No expenditure is questioned, no rumor is printed, no secret is revealed."

— President John F. Kennedy

Kennedy's words reveal that even decades ago, leaders recognized **the interlocking *network of political, financial, and media influence* shaping *public perception.***

Who Controls the Media?

Few realize that just six corporations control approximately 90% of U.S. media content — including what Americans read, watch, and hear. By 2011, these conglomerates dominated the industry:

- GE/Comcast – NBC, Universal
- News Corp – Fox News, Wall Street Journal, New York Post
- Disney – ABC, ESPN, Pixar
- Viacom – MTV, BET, Paramount Pictures
- Time Warner – CNN, HBO, Warner Bros.
- CBS Corporation – Showtime, NFL.com

This concentration of ownership means that most mainstream narratives are filtered through a handful of corporate and political interests. The media, in turn, discourages citizens from looking behind the curtain — urging passive consumption instead of critical thought.

A powerful quote from **John Swinton**, former Chief of Staff at *The New York Times* (1860–1870), captures this dynamic perfectly:

"There is no such thing, at this date of the world's history, in America, as an independent press. You know it and I know it. There is

99

not one of you who dares to write your honest opinions, and if you did, you know beforehand that it would never appear in print. I am paid weekly for keeping my honest opinion out of the paper I am connected with... The business of the journalist is to destroy the truth, to lie outright, to pervert, to vilify, to fawn at the feet of mammon, and to sell his country and his race for his daily bread... We are the tools and vassals of rich men behind the scenes. We are the jumping jacks; they pull the strings, and we dance. Our talents, our possibilities, and our lives are all the property of other men. We are intellectual prostitutes."

Swinton's words remain one of the most brutally honest confessions ever made about corporate journalism.

Global Perceptions and Modern Realities

Many nations outside the United States have also observed the **decline of American media integrity. President Vladimir Putin** once remarked: "Either the media don't understand the damage they're doing to their own country, in which case they are simply stupid, or they understand everything, in which case they are dangerous and corrupt."

When world leaders recognize this corruption, one must *ask: why do so few Americans see it themselves?*

Decades earlier, **Albert Einstein** foresaw the same pattern. In May 1949, he warned that **private capital would one day control all major channels of communication**, rendering true democracy almost impossible:

"Private capital tends to become concentrated in few hands, resulting in an oligarchy of private capital, the enormous power of which cannot be effectively checked even by a democratically organized political society... Under existing conditions, private capitalists inevitably control, directly or indirectly, the main sources of information — press, radio, and education. It is thus extremely difficult, and indeed in most cases quite impossible, for the individual citizen to come to objective conclusions and to make intelligent use of his political rights."

Einstein also declared:

"Blind belief in authority is the greatest enemy of truth."

Similarly, **Mark Twain** captured the irony of public information when he said:

"If you don't read the newspaper, you are uninformed. If you do read the newspaper, you are misinformed."

The Engine of Misinformation

Today, the line between truth and propaganda has become increasingly blurred. The rapid flow of information through television, print, and digital media has created an environment where narratives can be shaped, manipulated, or suppressed with alarming ease. When 99 government agencies hold influence over mainstream media, the stories presented to the public often reflect selective truths rather than objective reality. Independent journalists, whistleblowers, and alternative news platforms that challenge these official accounts are quickly branded as sources of "misinformation" or "conspiracy." This pattern of reflexive censorship not only protects those in power but also cultivates a culture of fear and self-censorship, where individuals hesitate to question what they are told.

As William Casey, the 13th Director of the CIA under President Reagan, once stated, "We'll know our disinformation program is complete when everything the American public believes is false." Whether this quote was meant literally or symbolically, it captures a profound truth about how perception can be engineered. When falsehoods are repeated often enough, they begin to resemble truth, and once the public accepts illusion as reality, control becomes effortless. In such a world, independent thought becomes an act of rebellion, and the search for truth turns into a moral duty rather than a mere intellectual pursuit.

The Sheep Mentality and the Loss of Power

People must understand that **blind obedience to authority** is the mechanism through which individual power is surrendered. By uncritically accepting governmental narratives, citizens give away their **innate capacity for discernment** — their "divine power."

The government's objective is to cultivate a **passive, compliant population**, one that follows orders rather than questions them. This suppression of critical thinking prevents collective resistance. We saw such resistance during the late 1960s, when citizens rose in protest against the Vietnam War. Today, similar dissent is methodically discouraged through censorship, distraction, and propaganda.

Every time individuals submit to unquestioned authority, they weaken their own sovereignty. As a result, the population becomes like sheep — obedient, fearful, and dependent.

To restore democracy as envisioned by the Founding Fathers, people must **reclaim their intellectual independence**. Awareness, critical thought, and the courage to question authority are the foundations upon which true freedom rests.

Chapter 27

Echelon: Invasion of Privacy

I've always known that everything we post online goes somewhere — the cloud, the servers, the data centers — but what most people don't realize is that it's not just social media companies watching us. Our own government has a secretive surveillance system known as **ECHELON**, originally a classified project under **the UK-USA Security Agreement**, which includes the **United States, Australia, Canada, New Zealand, and the United Kingdom** — the alliance we now call the **Five Eyes** *(Agent131711, Shadowbannedlibrary.com)*. It started back in the **late 1960s**, supposedly to keep tabs on military communications and diplomats, but over time, it evolved into something far bigger — a system capable of monitoring ordinary people like you and me.

Here's where it gets more disturbing. ECHELON has a "dictionary" — a keyword database that flags any conversation containing certain trigger words. Once a flagged word is used, that conversation is immediately recorded, downloaded, and reviewed (Agent131711, Shadowbannedlibrary.com). So while we go about chatting or sending messages, thinking we're just venting or joking, there's a silent algorithm sorting through our words and deciding whether we're worth listening to.

Then there's **FEMA's Red/Blue List**, which the government continues to deny even exists. They've slapped the "conspiracy theory" label on it to discourage anyone from looking deeper.

But when I started digging the work of **Agent131711**, co-founder of **Shadowbannedlibrary.com**, things started to line up. According to him, back in the **1980s**, FEMA and the military ran **mass-arrest drills** — simulations of quickly transforming military bases into detainment camps, rounding **up as many as half a million people at once** (Agent131711, Shadowbannedlibrary.com). That's not something you practice unless you plan to use it.

By 1997, the House of Representatives had quietly created **a Civilian Inmate Labor Camp document**, establishing policies for converting Army installations into prison camps for civilians. It's officially funded and staffed but kept out of public circulation (House of Representatives, 1997). Then, in **2002, Attorney General John Ashcroft** introduced the idea that any American labelled an **"enemy combatant"** could be detained indefinitely — without charge, without judicial oversight. And when you look at the vague definition of "enemy combatant," which basically includes anyone opposing U.S. policy or interests, it's easy to see how broad and dangerous that is (Ashcroft, 2002).

It didn't stop there. The **2006 Military Commissions Act** gave the government the legal power to imprison not only foreign suspects but also American citizens indefinitely, again without charge. By **2008,**

Halliburton's subsidiary KBR had secured an open-ended contract to construct **detention centers for Homeland Security.** And in **2009, Bill HR 645** authorized at least six **"National Emergency Centers"** to be built on military bases across the country — all away from public view (HR 645, 2009).

Around that same time, President **Barack Obama** publicly acknowledged the concept of **Prolonged Detention** — holding individuals not for what they've done, but for what the government suspects they might do in the future (Obama, 2009). That same year, **FM 3-39.40: Internment and Resettlement Operations, a Department of Defense manual**, was published, outlining how civilians could be detained, relocated, and "re-educated" to align with government-approved political views (DoD, 2010).

When **Senators John McCain and Joseph Lieberman** later introduced the **Enemy Belligerent, Interrogation, Detention, and Prosecution Act of 2010**, it confirmed what many of us had feared — that the U.S. military could detain citizens indefinitely without trial based solely on "suspected activity." No proof, no trial, just suspicion (McCain & Lieberman, 2010).

So, tell me again — does the **Red/Blue List** sound like a wild conspiracy theory? Because to me, the pieces fit too well to ignore. If you're on the **Red List**, FEMA comes for you — execution, no questions asked. If you're on the **Blue List**, you're rounded up and sent to a concentration camp. As extreme as that sounds, it's consistent with decades of quiet policy-building and legal groundwork. I believe it's not just possible — it's planned. That's why I keep telling people: reach out to your representatives, pray for guidance, and most of all, educate your families and friends. Awareness might be the only defense we have left (Agent131711, Shadowbannedlibrary.com).

Chapter 28

Proof of a Conspiracy to Kill President John F. Kennedy

Even after all these years, people still debate whether the assassination of **President John F. Kennedy** was a lone act or part of a deeper conspiracy. Personally, I've seen enough evidence to believe it was an orchestrated **coup d'état by the Military-Industrial Complex** — a coordinated effort to eliminate a president who had become a threat to entrenched power structures (House Select Committee on Assassinations, 1979).

For instance, the doctors at **Parkland Hospital** testified that the fatal wound on Kennedy's head was at the **rear occipital area**, suggesting **a shot from the front**, not from behind, where **Lee Harvey Oswald** supposedly stood (Parkland Testimonies, 1963). Add to that the impossible timing — Oswald had to fire three accurate shots from a poorly maintained rifle, from an awkward position, through branches of the Texas Live Oaks, all in just a few seconds. Even the **Warren Commission** admitted Oswald was a **"rather poor shot"** when he served in the Marines (Warren Commission Report, 1964).

Later, the **House Select Committee on Assassinations** officially concluded that **"President Kennedy was probably assassinated as a result of a conspiracy"**, though they stopped short of naming names

(House Select Committee on Assassinations, 1979). But I think the evidence points to something much larger. **Allen Dulles**, whom Kennedy fired as **CIA Director**, had motive enough — Kennedy had vowed to "break the CIA into a thousand pieces and scatter it to the wind." Combine that with Kennedy's efforts to challenge the **Federal Reserve** and his resistance to certain foreign interests, and you can see how he became a target (Hooker, 1963).

JFK alienated three of the most powerful entities in the world: the **CIA, Organised Crime, and the Israeli lobby**. These groups, often intertwined, had a shared interest in preserving their influence. His moves toward peace, his push for transparency, and especially his **Executive Order #11110**, which authorized the U.S. Treasury to issue **silver-backed currency**, directly threatened the **Federal Reserve's** control over money creation (Kennedy, 1963).

Think about that for a second. Kennedy effectively signed a document that allowed the U.S. to print its own money — interest-free — bypassing the Fed. More than **$4 billion in United States Notes** were printed, some even circulated briefly before being pulled after his death. I've personally held one of those 1963 two-dollar and five-dollar notes marked "United States Note", not "Federal Reserve Note." That alone speaks volumes. It's proof that Kennedy's order wasn't symbolic — it was already in motion (Kennedy, 1963).

And then, almost immediately after his assassination, the issuance of silver certificates stopped. Executive Order #11110 was quietly shelved. The timing says everything. Those who profit from the Federal Reserve's monopoly had every reason to ensure that Kennedy's reforms never saw the light of day. Even **Joseph P. Kennedy**, the president's father, once told **DeWest Hooker** that the family's ultimate goal was to "destroy the Rothschild-dominated Federal Reserve" (Hooker, 1963).

So when people say, "Oh, it's just a conspiracy theory," I can't help but shake my head. The facts, the motives, and the outcomes all point in one direction. The CIA's manipulation of the term **"conspiracy theory"** itself was part of their psychological operation — meant to discredit anyone questioning the official story (CIA Dispatch 1035-960, 1967). To me, it's not just a theory. It's history rewritten by those who benefit most from keeping the truth buried.

I've learned that Vice President Johnson (LBJ) seemed to know about President Kennedy's assassination before it even happened. He really didn't like Kennedy, and from what I've gathered, the comments he made to a woman revealed that he was aware the CIA was going to kill JFK (Coleman, 1992). There were two shooters that day, firing from the grassy knoll. Lee Harvey Oswald was just the patsy, set up to take the fall, while Jack Ruby — a CIA contract killer — was sent in to silence him (Coleman, 1992).

I don't believe Oswald could have shot Kennedy from the building where he was arrested. Coleman, an intelligence officer, claimed the British Monarchy itself was behind the killing of JFK (Coleman, 1992). Henry Kissinger was also involved in planning the setup for Kennedy's death. Two Dallas police officers who questioned two men in suits at the grassy knoll said those men claimed they were investigating the assassination. Film footage later confirmed that those same officers identified the men as likely shooters (House Select Committee on Assassinations, 1979).

According to top-secret classified documents, those two men who flashed FBI badges were actually the assassins. Based on Coleman's testimony, the British Monarchy ordered Kennedy's assassination (Coleman, 1992).

Chapter 29

9/11 -Proof it was Engineered

I've always found the official story of 9/11 absurd — full of physical impossibilities. The Twin Towers were designed to withstand the impact of a plane, something proven back in 1945 when a B-25 bomber crashed into the Empire State Building and it remained standing (Harrit et al., 2009). The idea that every vertical support failed simultaneously, resulting in a perfectly symmetrical collapse, is statistically impossible. For that to happen three times in one day, in one city, defies logic.

The towers didn't fall because of fire or planes. They came down through controlled demolition using strategically placed explosives; witnesses even heard explosions before the collapse (Jones, 2006). Both the Pentagon and the field crash were the result of scalar beam weaponry. The Pentagon section hit was where a communications unit had just moved. There was no footage of a large plane, and eyewitnesses didn't see one. The damage was far too specific — more like a missile strike (Lindauer, 2010).

Many people were warned not to show up for work on 9/11. Standard intercept procedures for hijacked planes were ignored, and the wreckage was swiftly cleared away. No plane debris or bodies were recovered at the Pentagon, and the black boxes — designed to survive such impacts — were said to be destroyed (Bowman, 2005).

Former CIA intelligence asset Susan Lindauer revealed that 9/11 was orchestrated by the CIA and Mossad (Lindauer, 2010). She was jailed without trial and told to keep quiet but later wrote Extreme Prejudice detailing her experience. New York fire lieutenant Paul Isaac Jr. confirmed that both police and firefighters knew it was an inside job but stayed silent out of fear.

Brigham Young physicist Steven Jones proved that thermite — and later nano-thermite — was used to cut through steel columns (Jones, 2006; Harrit et al., 2009). Even the Pentagon's impact raised questions: witnesses like pilot Samuel Danner said it wasn't a plane but a drone-like object, possibly a cruise missile, and radiation levels that day were abnormally high (Danner, 2007).

Captain Russ Wittenberg, U.S. Air Force, stated that there was no wreckage from a Boeing 757 at the Pentagon and that the official story was complete nonsense (Wittenberg, 2004). Over 1,400 cars melted near the WTC, something no plane crash could cause, indicating advanced energy weaponry (Wood, 2008). Seismic data even showed two massive explosions before the towers fell, followed by a smaller one from the plane's impact (Jones, 2006).

Building 7 — which wasn't hit by anything — collapsed perfectly in free fall. The BBC reported its fall half an hour before it actually happened (Harrit et al., 2009). Mark Loizeaux, president of Controlled Demolition Inc., said molten steel was found at the site weeks later. Structural engineer Leslie Robertson confirmed the fires were still burning and molten metal still flowing 21 days after the attacks (Robertson, 2001).

Attorney David Schippers said he sent details of the coming attacks to Attorney General Ashcroft, information he got from FBI agents told to stand down (Schippers, 2002). On top of that, suspicious "put options" were made on airline stocks right before the attacks — betting they'd crash (Bowman, 2005).

As Lt. Col. Robert Bowman (2005) said, "Scholars and professionals have established beyond any reasonable doubt that the official account of 9/11 is false." And I believe he was right — people were deceived by the very system they trusted.

Chapter 30

The Threat of the Oligarchy and Private Capital

The following is an editorial I wrote that was published in the Denver Post.

The book **"1984" by George Orwell** was written as a warning of what could happen if people allowed their governments to obtain too much power. The book also demonstrates the ability of governments to alter reality and manipulate facts to suit their narrative. "1984" is based on a dystopian vision of the future where the freedom of the individual is subjugated to the conformity of society."

His novel warns against the rise of authoritarian figures who charm and beguile us into exchanging our freedoms for the easier life of letting Big Government take over. George Orwell's vision of a dystopian world is most disturbing not because of its absurdities but because of the parallels that are now a part of our government. Please note that in some parts of our country this book is being banned. You need to question why is this book is being banned.

Chapter 31

U.S. Government spends billions on propaganda

I've come across something that really opened my eyes — the U.S. government has been spending billions just to shape public opinion. According to Stiles, between 2007 and 2015, the federal government poured over $4 billion into public relations services and another $2.2 billion into polling, research, and market consulting (Stiles, 2016). That's not chump change. It makes me wonder — why would a government that's supposed to be "of the people, by the people, for the people" need that kind of PR budget?

The answer seems obvious now: it's not about informing us; it's about conditioning us. The globalist cabal has been running one of the biggest cons in modern history — a deception so massive that most people still can't wrap their heads around it (Stiles, 2016). They've wormed their way into universities, scientific circles, and practically every branch of government, not just in the U.S. but worldwide.

What's worse is how completely the mainstream media has been hijacked. It's no longer about truth or free speech — it's about carefully curated narratives crafted by PR firms working for the global elite (Coleman, 1992). The "news" isn't news anymore; it's programming. It's designed to make people believe exactly what they're told, without question.

And if that sounds far-fetched, just listen to what one member of a very powerful family once said — someone whose name alone influences the world's direction. His arrogance makes it clear: they don't even hide their control anymore. They think we're too distracted to notice. You need to take very seriously what has been stated. You need to wake up to the fact that you have been conned and mind-controlled by the media.

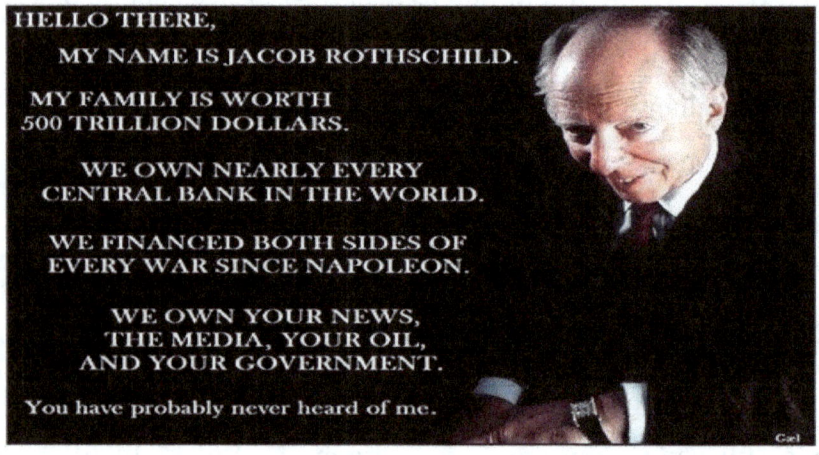

HELLO THERE,
MY NAME IS JACOB ROTHSCHILD.

MY FAMILY IS WORTH
500 TRILLION DOLLARS.

WE OWN NEARLY EVERY
CENTRAL BANK IN THE WORLD.

WE FINANCED BOTH SIDES OF
EVERY WAR SINCE NAPOLEON.

WE OWN YOUR NEWS,
THE MEDIA, YOUR OIL,
AND YOUR GOVERNMENT.

You have probably never heard of me.

Gæl

You need to take very seriously what has been stated. You need to wake up to the fact that you have been conned and mind-controlled by the media.

Chapter 32

Alternative Natural Energy Sources

I remember first reading about Stan Meyer and thinking, how could one man get so close to changing the entire energy game? Meyer's story really struck a chord with me. He wasn't some random tinkerer chasing impossible dreams. He attended Ohio State University, served in the military, and held several patents across diverse fields, including oceanography, cardiac monitoring, and banking systems (Meyer, 1993). His background alone painted the picture of someone with genuine scientific and technical depth. He even collaborated with NASA on the Gemini project and worked with the Battelle Foundation in Ohio. These weren't casual affiliations; they demonstrated that Meyer had credibility in circles that demand results, not speculation.

Alongside his brother Stephen, who served as an engineer in the United States Air Force, Meyer built up a thriving operation worth millions. He secured at least twelve patents, several of which fell under section 101—a classification that requires the inventor to physically prove functionality before approval. The fact that the U.S. Patent Office approved his application in just eight months, during a time when the system was notoriously slow, is telling. It implies that his invention was not only legitimate but compelling enough to attract immediate attention.

Meyer's claim was revolutionary. He said he had developed a "water fuel cell," registered under patent number US4389981A, that could separate hydrogen and oxygen from water with far less energy than conventional electrolysis. If true, this would have shattered the foundational principles of modern energy economics.

His demonstrations were not confined to backrooms or small-town fairs; they took place before respected experts like Professor Michael Laughton and Admiral Sir Anthony Griffin in London. Both men confirmed that Meyer's system produced far more hydrogen than expected under normal conditions. It is astonishing to imagine a vehicle traveling cross-country powered by nothing but twenty gallons of tap water (Laughton, 1993).

Yet, as history often shows, transformative discoveries rarely survive unchallenged. The moment Meyer's work began to gain traction, the tone surrounding him changed. In 1998, during a dinner with his brother Stephen and two Belgian investors, Meyer raised his glass of cranberry juice—and moments later, he collapsed, choking and gasping for air. His final words were chilling: "They poisoned me." That was his dying declaration." Stanley Meyer's bizarre death at age 57 ended his work. The man who claimed to have discovered a path to limitless clean energy was gone within minutes, and with him, possibly, a technology that could have altered the course of human civilization.

When I look at how the oil industry operates, none of this feels surprising. These corporations have spent decades defending their control over global energy markets. Any innovation that threatens their dominance tends to vanish from public view, often buried under technical disputes, patent buyouts, or mysterious circumstances. Free and abundant energy would dissolve the economic hierarchies that depend on scarcity and dependence. That kind of liberation would shift power away from a select few and back into the hands of ordinary people. So it makes sense that the so-called "global elite" would resist such change by any means necessary (Coleman, 1999).

Stan Meyer's legacy, whether misunderstood genius or silenced visionary, continues to challenge the boundaries of what we believe possible. His story is not just about science; it is about courage, suppression, and the lengths to which power will go to preserve control.

Chapter 33

The U.S. Navy Secret Alternative Energy Source

Now, here's something that really blows my mind. Back in 2014, Commander Randy shared something extraordinary—a breakthrough from the U.S. Navy that could have rewritten the entire global energy script. They had discovered a method to turn seawater into usable fuel (Randy, 2014). Yes, seawater, the most abundant resource on Earth, is transformed into energy that could power engines, ships, and aircraft. According to the U.S. Naval Research Laboratory, this fuel could be produced for roughly three to six dollars a gallon, and they had already demonstrated it successfully by flying a model aircraft powered entirely by this new energy source. Think about that for a moment. A branch of the U.S. military literally created fuel out of the ocean—and yet almost no one was talking about it.

The process itself is both elegant and groundbreaking. It involves extracting carbon dioxide and hydrogen directly from seawater using an electrolytic cation exchange module, or E-CEM for short. These two elements are then recombined through a metal catalyst to create liquid hydrocarbons—the basic building blocks of fuel (U.S. Naval Research Laboratory, 2014). In plain language, it is a closed-loop, carbon-neutral process that transforms ocean water into an energy source without adding pollution. The ocean already absorbs vast amounts of CO_2, so by using this technology, the system effectively recycles greenhouse gases while producing energy. It is one of the rare innovations that could clean the planet and power it at the same time.

But the question that lingers is simple and unsettling. If this technology truly exists and works as demonstrated, why isn't it being used everywhere? How could something this monumental barely make a blip in mainstream headlines? You would expect a discovery that converts seawater into fuel to dominate the news cycle for months, maybe even years. Instead, it quietly faded into the background, as if someone deliberately turned the volume down. The implications are too significant to ignore. With this kind of technology, nations could end their dependence on Middle Eastern oil entirely. Imagine the ripple effect: no more oil wars, no more excuses for military interventions, and no more geopolitical manipulation built around energy scarcity.

Commander Randy made a statement that still echoes with an uncomfortable truth. He said, "This will devastate oil-rich countries, but it will get us the hell out of the Middle East." His words cut through the noise of decades of political rhetoric. For years, wars have been sold to the public under the banners of "freedom," "security," or "fighting terrorism." Yet beneath those slogans lies an undeniable thread—the control of oil, the lifeblood of global power.

It's almost poetic in its irony. The very technology that could reduce human suffering, end conflicts over resources, and heal the environment has been kept in the shadows. It makes you wonder who truly benefits from the ongoing chaos and scarcity. Perhaps it is not about what humanity can achieve, but about what certain powers are willing to suppress to maintain control. The ability to make fuel from seawater should have been a story of hope, progress, and unity. Instead, it serves as another reminder of how far we still are from transparency in the systems that shape our world.

Chapter 34

The Deep State -Proof of Its Existence

Every time I bring up the Deep State, people roll their eyes like I've been watching too many movies. But honestly, the evidence is everywhere once you actually start paying attention. I used to think it was just another conspiracy theory too. But the deeper I looked, the more I realized that the patterns were too consistent to dismiss. The same names, the same institutions, the same revolving doors between corporate boardrooms and government offices—it's all hiding in plain sight.

President Woodrow Wilson said it best: *"Since I entered politics, I have chiefly had men's views confided to me privately. Some of the biggest men in the United States, in the field of commerce and manufacturing, are afraid of somebody, are afraid of something. They know that there is a power somewhere so organized, so subtle, so watchful, so interlocked, so complete, so pervasive, that they had better not speak above their breath when they speak in condemnation of it.* (Wilson, 1913).

That doesn't sound like paranoia. That sounds like a confession from someone who had seen behind the curtain. When a sitting president openly admits that there is a hidden power operating beyond public control, it forces you to wonder just how deep those roots go.

Then, in 1954, Senator William Jenner stood before Congress and issued a stark warning:

"Today the path to total dictatorship in the U.S. can be laid by strictly legal means ... We have a well-organized political-action group in this country, determined to destroy our Constitution and establish a one-party state. It operates secretly, silently, continuously to transform our Government. This ruthless power-seeking elite is a disease of our century. This group is answerable neither to the President, the Congress, nor the courts. It is practically irremovable."

Looking at today's landscape—corporate lobbyists writing laws, 123 unelected bureaucrats shaping policy, and global think tanks like the World Economic Forum or the Council on Foreign Relations influencing governments—it's hard not to see his words as prophecy. Decades later, we are living in the exact conditions he feared.

Even President Teddy Roosevelt, one of the most outspoken leaders in American history, exposed the same reality over a century ago: *"Behind the ostensible government sits enthroned an invisible government owing no allegiance and acknowledging no responsibility to the people. To destroy this invisible government, to befoul the unholy alliance between corrupt business and corrupt politics is the first task of the statesmanship of today."*

Roosevelt was not known for exaggeration. His warning was a direct challenge to the banking and corporate powers already consolidating behind the scenes. He knew that unchecked economic influence would eventually lead to political control, and he was right.

And then, decades later, David Rockefeller himself—the patriarch of one of the most powerful families in modern history—admitted in his own memoirs that he and others were indeed working toward a more integrated global political and economic structure:

"Some people even believe we are part of a secret cabal working against the best interests of the United States, characterizing my family and me as 'internationalists' and of conspiring with others around the world to build a more integrated global political and economic structure, one world if you will. If that is the charge, I stand guilty, and I am proud of it."

This wasn't speculation. This was a declaration made in his own words, preserved in print for anyone willing to read it. When someone of that stature says it out loud, how can we still pretend it's fiction? Here is one last quote from Rockefeller: "We are on the verge of a global transformation. All we need is the right major crisis and the Nations will accept the New World Order."

We have been sold the illusion of democracy while the true levers of power operate quietly in the background. It's like living in a massive psychological Matrix, a system so vast and well-designed that most people never even question it. The media distracts, the schools indoctrinate, and the financial institutions ensure dependency. The Rockefeller and Rothschild dynasties have shaped the foundations of both the European and American banking systems for centuries. Their influence extends through oil, media, pharmaceuticals, and even education. Generations of control have allowed them to build a network so deeply embedded in the global framework that it no longer needs to hide.

The most unsettling part is that none of this is truly secret anymore. The information is out there—available to anyone who chooses to look—but the conditioning runs so deep that most dismiss it instantly. The label "conspiracy theorist" has become a convenient tool for silencing curiosity. But at this point, denying the existence of the Deep State feels less like skepticism and more like willful blindness. Everything that was once mocked or ridiculed as fantasy is gradually being confirmed, piece by piece, unfolding right in front of us. The truth has never been hidden. It has simply been disguised as nonsense until it becomes too obvious to ignore.

Further Proof of the Deep State's Grip

When I first came across J. Edgar Hoover's quote, I had to read it twice. This man wasn't just anyone—he was the first Director of the FBI and held that position for 48 years. He had eyes and ears everywhere, and access to intelligence that even Congress couldn't touch. So when Hoover said, *"The individual is handicapped by coming face-to-face with a conspiracy so monstrous he cannot believe it exists... It rejects even the assumption that human creatures could espouse a philosophy that must ultimately destroy all that is good and decent,"* (Hoover, 1956).

This message sent chills down my back. That's not a random warning—it's an insider telling us flat-out what's going on behind the curtain.

And Hoover wasn't the only one. Even President Bill Clinton once admitted, *"There's a government inside the government, and I don't control it."* (Clinton, 1993). That's one of those statements that slips out, gets buried, and is never mentioned again—but it says everything. The so-called leaders we vote for? They're just front men for something much bigger and much darker.

These "invisible" forces—especially the international bankers and the Rockefeller Standard Oil empire—have controlled the press for decades. They own most of the newspapers and use them to silence or drive out anyone who refuses to play along (Rockefeller, 2003). It's like an unspoken rule: cross them, and you're finished.

Paul Warburg, who sat on the Council on Foreign Relations, even told the U.S. Senate Committee on Foreign Relations back in 1950, *"We shall have world government, whether or not you like it. The question is only whether world government will be achieved by consent or by conquest."* (Warburg, 1950). That one line says it all. They weren't hiding their intentions—they were just banking on the fact that people wouldn't believe them.

Now, this next part might sound extreme to anyone who hasn't done the digging, but it's impossible to ignore once you start connecting the dots. The Deep State isn't just political— it's satanic at its core. These people maintain their power through propaganda, censorship, financial manipulation, and, shockingly, ritualistic child sacrifice (Coleman, 1999). I know how insane that sounds, but the deeper you look, the more disturbing it gets. Even the FDA, believe it or not, has turned a blind eye to practices that cross the line into the grotesque.

At the top of all this sits what many researchers call the Khazarian Mafia—an elite group with roots tracing back centuries. Their goal? A one-world government, a Luciferian control grid where every nation loses its sovereignty under their centralized rule (Rockefeller, 2003). It's an agenda so deeply woven into politics, finance, and culture that most people can't even see it. But once you do, there's no unseeing it.

And here's what I keep reminding myself: they thrive on division. *"United we stand, divided we fall"* isn't just a cliché—it's their biggest fear. The Deep State knows that if people ever truly came together, their whole empire would crumble overnight. They keep us fighting, distracted, and divided so we never notice the puppet strings. But awareness is spreading. Slowly, people are waking up—and that terrifies them.

I recently found this cartoon that is very prophetic.

Chapter 35

HAARP - A Weaponized Weather System

The first time I heard about HAARP, I thought it sounded too wild to be real. But the deeper I dug, the more I realized just how much the U.S. government has gone out of its way to bury this truth. They want us to think it's all a myth—a "conspiracy theory." But the evidence says otherwise.

HAARP, or the **High-Frequency Active Auroral Research Program**, began in 1993 and sits in the rugged wilderness of **Gakona, Alaska**. From the outside, it looks like a simple grid of antennas spread across frozen terrain, but these antennas emit **high-frequency radio waves** directly into the ionosphere—the layer of Earth's upper atmosphere that influences weather and communication. The official story is that it's all about "studying auroras." The reality is far more dangerous (Begich, 1995).

Even **Dr. Peter Vincent Pry**, a respected national security expert, warned about the rise of *"weaponized weather."* He said countries could use weather as a weapon to **cripple U.S. power grids**—no missiles, no bombs, just engineered storms that cause blackouts and chaos (Pry, 2019). Pry called it a potential *"blackout war,"* where extreme weather is combined with cyberattacks, EMPs, and sabotage to collapse entire infrastructures—communications, food supply, transportation, even emergency services.

What most people don't know is that HAARP is only one piece of a **global network.** It's part of the so-called **Super Dual Auroral Radar Network Highway**—an array of high-frequency radars stretching across both hemispheres. In other words, this isn't just one installation in Alaska—it's an interconnected system capable of manipulating atmospheric conditions on a planetary scale (Global Research, 2007).

In the book *Angels Don't Play This HAARP*, co-author **Dr. Nick Begich** revealed that the system's technology evolved from **Tesla's theories**—ideas that focused on manipulating electromagnetic fields for energy transmission and, disturbingly, for mind control and weather modification (Begich & Manning, 1995). Begich explained how HAARP could **transfer massive amounts of energy** to pinpointed areas using **Artificial Ionospheric Mirrors (AIMs)**—essentially reflective energy conduits created in the sky.

According to multiple outlets—including *E Magazine, Pravda, Wired*, and **Global Research**—HAARP's potential effects go far beyond "climate research." It's allegedly capable of **inducing droughts, floods, hurricanes, earthquakes, volcanic eruptions, and even disabling aircraft and satellites** by disrupting their electronic systems (Wired, 2003; Global Research, 2007). These claims align uncomfortably well with the U.S. military's stated goal of developing "weather warfare" technologies.

Even **Professor Michel Chossudovsky**, founder of *Global Research*, stated plainly that HAARP is *"part of the weapons arsenal of* *the New World Order*." He warned that entire economies could be destabilized through **climatic manipulation**, and nations wouldn't even realize they were under attack until it was too late (Chossudovsky, 2009).

The U.S. Air Force itself published a report titled *Weather as a Force Multiplier*, describing how controlling the weather could give "warfighters" an edge in future conflicts. They talked about "dominance of global communications" and "counter-space control" through atmospheric modification—a chilling confirmation that this is about control, not science (USAF, 1996).

Then there's **the acoustic and electromagnetic side** of it. In 2001, *Science and Global Security* reported that **infrasound**, a low-frequency wave that HAARP can generate, can cause **localized earthquakes**. The authors **Alvin and Heidi Toffler**, in their 1993 book *War and Antiwar*, wrote that electromagnetic weapons could be used to **trigger earthquakes and volcanic eruptions** (Toffler & Toffler, 1993).

Even Russia's military journals took notice. In January 2008, an online publication called Nuclearno.ru referred to HAARP as a **"geophysical weapon disguised as a research facility"**, capable of destroying entire economies or destabilizing nations through engineered seismic and weather events (Nuclearno.ru, 2008).

So, when the government dismisses HAARP as harmless "research," remember: they've been caught lying before. What's happening in Alaska—and across the global radar network—isn't science for the sake of progress. It's science for the sake of control. And if you control the weather, you control the world. This is a picture of what HAARP looks like

Chapter 36

Federal Reserve and the IRS are Illegal Entities

I've spent years studying the truth about our monetary system, and the deeper I dug, the more unsettling the truth became. The Federal Reserve is not a government agency designed to safeguard the American people; it's a private banking cartel, owned and controlled by a small circle of international financiers. It functions independently of the U.S. government, answers to no electorate, and yet it dictates the value of every dollar we earn, spend, and save. Each note printed under its authority is, in essence, a debt instrument — not a symbol of wealth, but a receipt of obligation.

The illusion began on December 23, 1913, when President Woodrow Wilson signed the Federal Reserve Act. I often imagine that moment — a quiet signing, just before Christmas, when most of Congress had already left Washington. With that single act, the sovereignty of America's money was handed over to private interests. That day, without a shot fired, the financial destiny of an entire nation was sold. Wilson himself would later lament, "I have unwittingly ruined my country," acknowledging the enormity of the mistake.

If ordinary Americans truly understood that our currency is issued by a private corporation that profits from every dollar of debt we owe, there would be outrage on a scale this nation has never seen. As Senator Barry Goldwater once warned, *"The accounts of the Federal Reserve*

System have never been audited. It operates outside the control of Congress and manipulates the credit of the United States." And it still does.

Even centuries earlier, Thomas Jefferson foresaw the danger. "Banking institutions are more dangerous to our liberties than standing armies," he said, cautioning that the power to issue and control money should never rest in private hands. Yet here we are, more than two hundred years later, enslaved by precisely that system. Every tax payment, every interest charge, every inflationary surge — all of it feeds the same engine of debt.

The IRS, for its part, serves as the enforcement arm of this machinery. Its partnership with the Federal Reserve is not accidental but deliberate. I was very fortunate to have accidentally stumbled upon a copy of the IRS Handbook titled *"Special Agents – Criminal Investigation Intelligence Division"*. Note that nobody outside of the IRS is allowed to have this book. On its cover, it read: *"Our tax system is based on self-assessment and voluntary compliance."* Note the word **voluntary**. A word that reveals more about the illusion of choice than most realize. The system depends not on law, but on obedience and fear — on the belief that resistance is futile.

And then there's **BlackRock** — the silent colossus. Founded by Larry Fink, it is the very embodiment of financial consolidation. Its AI system, Aladdin, built in 1988, now oversees and influences over $21 trillion in assets — a sum larger than the GDPs of the U.S. and China combined. Through Aladdin's data network, BlackRock effectively monitors and shapes the movement of global capital. It advises central banks, including the Federal Reserve itself, and wields unseen influence over everything from housing markets to energy policy.

It's no exaggeration to say that we are standing at the edge of a new kind of financial tyranny — one not enforced by armies, but by algorithms. A future where our money, homes, and even personal freedoms may be algorithmically managed under the guise of "efficiency."

This isn't freedom; it's servitude dressed up as progress. Every paycheck, every transaction, every so-called bailout brings us deeper into a web designed not to empower the people, but to keep them quietly indebted to those who own the system itself. The Federal Reserve was never America's protector — it was, from the beginning, its silent master.

Chapter 37

Washington DC – Is it a Corporation?

Here's something most people never realize — Washington D.C. isn't truly part of the United States in the way we've been taught. It stands apart as a separate corporate entity, operating under its own constitution, its own jurisdiction, and its own set of laws. This all traces back to the Act of 1871, a quiet yet monumental shift that redefined the federal government not as a representative Republic, but as a corporate structure. In essence, it turned the United States into a business — **THE UNITED STATES CORPORATION** — with citizens treated as assets rather than sovereign individuals.

When I first stumbled across this information, everything about the peculiar nature of D.C. suddenly made sense. It explains why the city functions like its own enclosed realm — where politicians, lobbyists, and bureaucrats live by a different set of rules. The residents of D.C. don't enjoy full representation like other Americans. Even their flag, with its three distinct red stars, seems symbolic: each star representing Washington D.C., the Vatican, and the City of London — the triad believed to form the backbone of a global power structure.

It's a striking idea: three independent city-states, each ruling a distinct sphere of control — **Washington D.C.** wielding military power, **London** commanding global finance, and the **Vatican** presiding over spiritual and moral influence. Together, they form what many call the "unholy trinity" of global governance — a power network not bound by national borders but by shared interests. Once you see it, you can't unsee it.

Technically, federal authority was meant to apply only within a ten-mile radius of the District of Columbia. Yet, over time, that authority crept outward, wrapping itself around the fifty states like a legal web. Through this gradual expansion, the federal system began treating the entire nation as an extension — a sub-corporation under the central corporate government.

Gerald Brown's *Cooperative Federalism* explores this dynamic in chilling detail, showing how the United States transformed into a "federal corporation" that manages people and resources like inventory. Reading it felt like someone had lifted a veil. Suddenly, the illusion of democracy looked more like a finely tuned system of economic and administrative control.

And when you connect this to the events of 1913 — the same year the Federal Reserve was established — the picture becomes even clearer. That year, Congress effectively handed over America's gold and silver reserves to the Rothschild-controlled banking network. From that point onward, the nation's wealth became a commodity traded by private interests, and our once-sovereign Republic slipped quietly into servitude.

So I can't help but ask the same question every time I look at the Capitol dome: Who does this government truly serve? The people? Or the corporation behind the curtain? Because if history has shown us anything, it's that the moment profit becomes the motive, the Republic ceases to be for the people — it becomes property

Chapter 38

The United States Flag with a Yellow Fringe is Unconstitutional

One day, I walked into a courtroom and noticed something odd — a **U.S. flag with a yellow fringe** around it. I remember thinking, "That doesn't look right." Later, I learned why.

Under **Title 4 of the United States Code**, the national flag is described in detail — but there's **no mention** of a yellow fringe. That fringe isn't decorative; it's symbolic. It represents **martial law** and **admiralty jurisdiction** — the law of the sea, not the law of the land.

Every courtroom that flies that yellow-fringed flag is effectively telling you that you're under military authority. And by standing there, you've silently agreed to it. It's chilling when you realize what that means — the Constitution we think protects us doesn't apply in that room.

In maritime law, the gold fringe signifies wartime status, and the tassels you see hanging from the pole? They're not just for show — they confirm the same thing. We are, quite literally, living under a perpetual state of martial control, disguised as civil governance.

Of course, if you check Wikipedia, it'll dismiss all of this as a conspiracy theory. But ask yourself — if it weren't true, why are those flags in every courtroom? Why won't the government explain their meaning under oath?

The truth is, they rely on our ignorance to keep this illusion alive. If the American people ever woke up to what those symbols really mean, there would be outrage overnight — and they can't afford that.

Chapter 39

Stargates -do they exist?

I decided to include this topic out of sheer curiosity—because, honestly, who hasn't wondered about it? My answer is simple: yes, stargates do exist. And no, I'm not talking about the kind you see in Hollywood blockbusters. I'm talking about something NASA itself has quietly acknowledged — natural "Earth portals" that connect distant regions of space in ways we're only beginning to understand.

In 2015, NASA confirmed that these portals—scientifically referred to as magnetic reconnection points—are real and have been under study for years. Using data from the **THEMIS spacecraft and the European Space Agency's Cluster probes**, researchers observed invisible energy gateways forming at specific locations around Earth. These portals typically emerge where our planet's **magnetic field** interacts with the solar wind, creating temporary "flux transfer events." In simpler terms, they open direct energy channels linking Earth to the Sun's magnetic field.

That same year, NASA launched the **Magnetospheric Multiscale Mission (MMS)**—a fleet of four spacecraft flying in tight formation— to investigate these phenomena more closely. The mission's goal was to map and understand how particles and energy move through these portals in real time. The findings revealed that these magnetic gateways can open and close multiple times per day, often with little warning, transferring enormous amounts of charged energy through space.

Now, while NASA's language is technical, the implications are fascinating. What ancient civilizations once described as "gates to the gods" or "windows to the heavens" might, in modern terms, be magnetic pathways bridging distant points in our solar environment. Whether we call them stargates, portals, or reconnection nodes, the underlying concept is eerily similar — natural, energetic doorways through which matter and energy flow across vast distances.

So, while mainstream science stops short of calling them "stargates" in the science fiction sense, the reality is every bit as compelling. These magnetic portals remind us that our planet is not isolated in space — it's part of a vast, dynamic system of energy currents that literally connect Earth to the Sun. Maybe, just maybe, what our ancestors called magic, we're only now learning to measure.

The Bermuda Triangle – Earth's Most Famous Stargate

Among all the alleged stargates on Earth, the **Bermuda Triangle** remains the most infamous and perplexing of them all. Stretching across the region bordered **by San Juan (Puerto Rico), Bermuda Island, and Miami (Florida)**, this triangular expanse—often referred to as the Devil's Triangle—has captivated the world's imagination for decades. It's not just a patch of ocean; it's a place where reality itself seems to bend.

Since the early 1950s, **an unsettling number of aircraft, naval vessels, and private boats** have disappeared within this mysterious zone, often without a trace or distress call. Entire crews have vanished as if swallowed by the sea, their ships later found adrift and empty. Even the most advanced technology—compasses, radios, radar—has been reported to fail abruptly in these waters.

In 1964, journalist **Vincent H. Gaddis** brought the phenomenon to public attention in his groundbreaking article, later expanded into a book, Invisible Horizons. He meticulously chronicled dozens of these unexplained vanishings and questioned why, despite so many incidents, **official investigations remained inconclusive or conveniently silent**. His work suggested a deliberate effort to suppress or dismiss deeper truths about what was really happening in that region.

Some theories propose that the Bermuda Triangle could be the location of **an active stargate or energy vortex**, a natural anomaly where magnetic and gravitational forces overlap, distorting space-time. Others believe it may be tied to lost technologies from ancient civilizations—perhaps remnants of Atlantis or unknown underwater installations.

What's undeniable is the pattern of secrecy that surrounds it. **Government agencies and military archives remain largely classified**, while independent researchers who pursue this mystery often face ridicule or obstruction. It's easier for those in power to label it all as "myth" or "coincidence" than to admit there are forces at play they can't fully control or explain.

Those who scoff at the idea of stargates in places like the Bermuda Triangle often haven't examined the evidence for themselves—or worse, they've fallen victim to the very information control systems designed to keep humanity unaware of the larger cosmic mechanisms operating around us. The truth may be stranger, and far closer, than we've been led to believe.

Chapter 40

The Phil Schneider Story – The Phil Schneider Story – Classified Secrets and the Hidden War

Phil Schneider's story is one of those accounts that, once you hear it, you can't easily shake off. He wasn't some fringe theorist or self-proclaimed whistleblower—he was a **highly qualified geological and structural engineer**, a man who worked directly with classified U.S. military projects. Holding a **Rhyolite-38 security clearance**, a level reportedly higher than that of most U.S. Presidents, Schneider had access to deep-level operations and black-budget programs that the general public never hears about.

According to his testimony, Schneider helped construct **deep underground military bases (DUMBs)** across the United States, the most notorious of which was the **Dulce Base** in New Mexico. Dulce has long been rumored to house joint human–extraterrestrial operations—experiments, genetic research, and technologies far beyond what's publicly acknowledged. Schneider claimed to have been physically present during a 1979 confrontation between U.S. military personnel and non-human entities in Dulce's lower levels—an encounter that allegedly left dozens dead.

When I attended his 1994 Denver lecture, Schneider spoke calmly, methodically, like a man with nothing left to lose. He presented slides, blueprints, and even fragments of what he described as advanced metal alloys—materials he said could not be reproduced with current Earth technology. His words carried the weight of someone who had lived under the shadow of secrecy for too long.

Seven months later, he was found dead in his apartment—strangled with piano wire, the official report ruling it a suicide. To those of us who had followed his work, the circumstances felt chillingly deliberate. Schneider had repeatedly said, "If I ever 'commit suicide,' you'll know I was murdered."

Before his death, he released several warnings about secret government operations, alien treaties, and underground networks that connected military installations from coast to coast. He believed a shadow government was preparing for a future event—something involving both human and non-human collaboration—and he wanted the world to know before it was too late.

Phil Schneider died trying to tell the truth as he saw it. Whether one believes every detail or not, his courage to speak out against overwhelming odds makes his story a cornerstone in the lore of modern disclosure. Even decades later, his message still echoes—**a reminder that the world beneath our feet may be far stranger than we've been led to believe.**

The 1979 Dulce Firefight

In 1979, Phil Schneider claimed to have experienced something that defies imagination. While working on a deep-level military construction project in **Dulce, New Mexico**, his team allegedly broke into an existing underground chamber—one not of human origin. What followed, he said, was a **firefight between government personnel and alien humanoids** that left sixty-six people dead. Schneider was one of only three survivors, and the only one who ever went public.

He described how he was **shot in the chest by a directed-energy weapon**, an alien device that burned through his body and left him permanently disfigured. The blast exposed him to **cobalt radiation**, which he believed led to his later battle with cancer. During his lectures, Schneider would lift his shirt and show the scars—raw, unmistakable evidence, he said, of what had happened that day.

But Schneider didn't stop there. He revealed what he called the **Black Budget**—a secret, unaccounted-for government fund that, in 1995, he estimated to exceed **$1.25 trillion annually.** This budget, he claimed, financed the construction of **129 deep underground military bases (DUMBs)** across the United States alone. Each base, he said, was **a vast subterranean complex**, equipped with advanced research facilities and connected by a nationwide network of magneto-leviton trains capable of reaching speeds of **Mach 2** or higher.

He painted a picture of a hidden world beneath our feet—a second America, built not for public knowledge or benefit, but for secret experiments, military operations, and interspecies collaboration. According to Schneider, these underground networks weren't science fiction—they were a shadow infrastructure, funded by taxpayers but concealed under the highest levels of classified secrecy.

When he spoke, Schneider didn't sound like a man telling stories. He sounded like someone unburdening himself of a truth too heavy to carry. Whether one accepts his claims or not, his conviction, evidence, and consistency left a deep mark on everyone who heard him. To this day, his story remains one of the most detailed and disturbing accounts ever linked to alleged government–extraterrestrial collaboration.

The Greada Treaty and Alien Collaboration

Back in 1954, during the Eisenhower administration, an alleged event took place that would become one of the most controversial claims in modern history. According to Phil Schneider and other whistleblowers, the U.S. government entered into a secret treaty with a non-human race—a pact known as the **Greada Treaty**. The story goes that representatives from the U.S. military and intelligence agencies met with **extraterrestrial beings** at Edwards Air Force Base, where the two sides reached an extraordinary agreement.

In exchange for access to advanced alien technology—energy systems, propulsion methods, and materials science decades beyond human capability—the government allegedly granted these beings permission to **abduct a limited number of humans and animals** for scientific research, on the condition that all subjects would be **returned safely and without memory of the event**.

But there was another offer on the table. A more benevolent group of extraterrestrials, said to come from the Pleiades star system, had also approached U.S. leaders. Their terms were different: they offered technological knowledge and spiritual wisdom—**but only if humanity agreed to dismantle its nuclear arsenal and renounce warfare**. The Eisenhower administration declined, unwilling to relinquish military dominance in a world still locked in the Cold War.

Schneider believed that the decision sealed our fate. The U.S. chose power over peace, aligning with entities whose motives were far from altruistic. Soon after, reports of **unexplained abductions** began to rise sharply. The supposed "dark" visitors ignored the limits of the agreement, taking humans at will, conducting experiments, and violating every condition of the original treaty.

By the late 1960s, the U.S. government had lost control of the situation entirely. What began as a technological exchange had spiraled into a **quiet invasion of human sovereignty**, hidden beneath the veil of national security. Schneider often said that this was the turning point—the moment when humanity's pursuit of control opened the door to forces it could no longer contain.

Whether viewed as myth, metaphor, or suppressed history, the Greada Treaty stands as a haunting parable of power, secrecy, and the peril of making deals with those we do not truly understand.

Government Cover-ups and False Flag Attacks

Schneider also claimed that, due to his extensive background in geological and explosive engineering, he was brought in to **investigate the 1993 World Trade Center bombing**. What he found, he said, defied the official explanation. According to Schneider, the pattern and extent of the structural damage **were inconsistent with a conventional truck bomb**. The shockwave signatures and the destruction beneath the building, he argued, pointed instead to a **small-scale nuclear device or a sophisticated underground explosive**, far beyond what any civilian group could have deployed.

He described the event as a deliberate act of deception—**a false flag operation designed to test controlled demolition technologies** and to gauge public reaction to a "terrorist" event on American soil. Schneider said that when he presented his findings to federal authorities, he was warned to stay silent and soon after found himself removed from the investigation.

He later drew parallels to the **1995 Oklahoma City bombing**, insisting that the narrative of a lone domestic terrorist using a fertilizer-based truck bomb was scientifically impossible. The damage pattern, especially the deep shearing of reinforced concrete columns, could not have been caused by an external explosion. Schneider claimed that **advanced internal charges or classified energy weapons** were used instead, with Timothy McVeigh positioned as the scapegoat to divert public scrutiny.

For Schneider, both incidents illustrated a chilling reality: that **certain factions within the government were using engineered tragedies to expand control, test covert technologies, and manipulate public sentiment**. Whether or not one accepts his conclusions, his courage to challenge official accounts—and the price he ultimately paid—has made his story one of the most haunting in the history of government secrecy.

Surveillance and Secret Weaponry

Schneider spoke often about the **massive and highly secretive militarisation of U.S. airspace**, revealing that more than **64,000 unmarked black helicopters** were already in operation within American borders. These helicopters, he said, were specially designed for **nighttime surveillance, rapid deployment, and covert extractions**, often seen flying at low altitudes without identification lights. According to him, their presence was not for national defense but **for domestic control and population monitoring**, part of a growing surveillance state hidden behind "national security."

He also disclosed the existence of **157 F-117A stealth aircraft**, many of which had been modified far beyond their published capabilities. These aircraft, he claimed, were equipped with **LIDAR systems and high-frequency radar imaging technology** capable of penetrating physical structures. "They can see right through your roof and into your home," Schneider warned, "from 30,000 miles away." The implication was clear—**privacy, as we understand it, no longer exists.**

But perhaps his most disturbing revelation was about **earthquake-inducing technology**. Drawing on Tesla's early experiments with vibrational resonance, Schneider claimed the government had perfected devices capable of generating seismic activity anywhere on the planet. He cited the **Kobe earthquake of 1995 and the San Francisco quake of 1989** as potential examples, pointing out that both lacked the usual electromagnetic pulse waves associated with natural seismic events. "These weren't acts of nature," he said. "They were demonstrations of power."

Whether viewed as whistleblowing or warning, Schneider's message carried the same underlying truth: **that technological control had surpassed public knowledge by decades**, and that those who wielded it no longer operated under the oversight of any elected authority.

Chapter 41

Chemtrails and the 5G Network

Now, let me confront two of the most controversial and deliberately dismissed topics of our time: **chemtrails and 5G radiation safety**. Society has been systematically conditioned to scoff at both—labeling them "conspiracy theories"—yet, behind this carefully managed narrative lies mounting evidence that challenges the official story.

Let's start with **5G**, the cornerstone of the coming digital surveillance era. **The U.S. government has never conducted a single comprehensive health study** to confirm the safety of 5G frequencies. Even more concerning, **mainstream media outlets have been issued informal gag directives**—discouraged from reporting on independent research that questions 5G's biological effects. The question arises: if there's nothing to hide, why the silence?

Interestingly, not every region has ignored the warnings. **Brussels, Russia, several Italian municipalities, Portland (Oregon), and**

Nevada City (California) have either **banned or suspended the 5G rollout**, citing health and environmental concerns. These are not isolated protests—they're the result of local governments responding to citizen outcry and independent data.

5G networks operate at **extremely high frequencies—between 24 GHz and 86 GHz**, well into the millimeter-wave spectrum. At these levels, signals don't just bounce off surfaces—**they interact with human biology**. Independent scientists have linked prolonged exposure to **reduced oxygen absorption in the blood, cellular stress, DNA fragmentation, sleep disruption, fertility issues, and elevated cancer risk**. The electromagnetic load on the human body is cumulative, and 5G, with its dense grid of transmitters, dramatically increases overall exposure.

The **World Health Organization (WHO)**, stated that there were serious illnesses related to exposure to EMF radiation from the 5G network. Here is what the World Health Organization says are some of the more serious illnesses caused by 5G.

In their report, they included the risk of damaging your DNA, disrupting sleep cycles, increasing stress levels and increasing the risk of cancer. Also, there is "strong prospective evidence that prenatal exposure to these magnetic fields above a certain level may be associated with miscarriage risk," as reported by Epidemiology. Yet another study was also published by Epidemiology that stated the fact that several studies were done that have identified occupational exposure to extremely low-frequency electromagnetic fields (EMF) as a potential risk factor for neuro-degenerative disease."

Ian Furgeson, who is a 5G technician who installs the 5G towers, stated that the 5G network is 15,000 times stronger than the current toxic radiation that we are exposed to.

Renowned experts such as **Dr. Ulrich Warnke, Dr. Magda Havas**, and **Dr. Keith Black** have all voiced serious concern. Dr. Black, a respected neurosurgeon, put it starkly: *"Microwave radiation essentially cooks the brain."* Dr. Ulrich Warnke, a former mobile phone industry insider, has linked EMF radiation to over 30 health conditions. With 5G's intensified pulse modulation and close-range emitters, that **thermal and biological effect becomes exponentially magnified.**

The truth is not in the denial—but in the data. And that data increasingly points to a technology being unleashed faster than science—or ethics—can keep up with.

Li-Fi – A Safer Alternative

Fortunately, there is hope—and it comes in the form of **a revolutionary technology known as Li-Fi (Light Fidelity).** Unlike traditional Wi-Fi, which relies on potentially harmful **radio frequency (RF) waves**, Li-Fi uses **visible light waves emitted from LED bulbs** to transmit data. The result is not only **blazing-fast connectivity and higher data capacity, but also complete safety for human biology**.

Li-Fi harnesses light, the purest and most natural form of energy. Because light cannot penetrate solid walls, **data transmission remains**

contained within individual rooms, creating an environment that is **virtually immune to external interference, hacking, or electromagnetic pollution.** This inherent limitation, often seen as a drawback, actually becomes Li-Fi's greatest strength—**ensuring privacy, data integrity, and security** in ways Wi-Fi could never achieve.

Already, **research labs and tech innovators across the globe** are testing Li-Fi in **industrial, commercial, and even aviation environments**, demonstrating its efficiency and stability. Early results suggest that Li-Fi can deliver speeds **up to 100 times faster than WiFi,** all while consuming less energy and emitting zero electromagnetic radiation.

If embraced on a global scale, Li-Fi could **redefine digital communication,** offering a future that is not only **smarter and faster** but also **healthier and more ecologically sound.** In a world increasingly saturated with wireless frequencies, **light itself may hold the key to our technological salvation.**

Chemtrails – The Truth Behind the Skies

Now, let's turn our attention to **chemtrails**—a topic that remains heavily misunderstood and dismissed by the mainstream. According to Wikipedia, contrails are "line-shaped clouds formed by aircraft engine exhaust or changes in air pressure at high altitudes," made primarily of ice crystals. But that explanation defies basic logic. **Ice crystals cannot**

linger in the sky for hours; atmospheric science confirms they should dissipate within minutes under normal conditions.

People have become so conditioned that they no longer see the difference between a **fleeting contrail and a lingering chemical trail**. The truth is, chemtrails are not a hoax. I've personally watched them stretch across the sky for hours—long after any vapor trail should have evaporated—forming hazy veils that dim sunlight and alter the atmosphere's clarity.

Independent researchers have conducted tests on air, soil, and groundwater samples collected beneath these trails. Their findings are deeply concerning: **toxic concentrations of heavy metals such as barium, cadmium, and nickel**—each with severe health implications.

- **Barium**, used in industrial applications and rodenticides, is linked to respiratory distress, heart irregularities, and paralysis.
- **Cadmium** contributes to heart disease, cancer, and kidney damage.
- **Nickel**, once introduced as a gasoline additive, has been associated with lung and nasal cancers.

These particles infiltrate our bodies through the air we breathe, the water we drink, and even through dermal absorption. Despite mounting evidence, government and military agencies continue to **deny any involvement**. Yet, there are **over 150 publicly available patents** detailing technologies for aerosolized nanoparticle dispersal.

To me, that denial speaks volumes. **Chemtrails are not mere theory—they are part of a larger system of control.** And the phrase *"conspiracy theory"* has become the most effective weapon for silencing those who dare to look up and ask questions.

Chapter 42

Climate Change — The True Cause

Next, I want to discuss something equally distorted by mainstream narratives: **climate change**. People have been relentlessly lied to about what's truly causing it. Throughout Earth's history, climate change has always been **a natural process.** Ancient records and geological data prove that warming and cooling cycles have occurred long before industrialization.

In the early 1960s, scientists were warning about an approaching **mini ice age**, not global warming. So, what changed? Not the Earth— our governments' agenda did.

Let's look at the evidence. Warming is happening **across the entire solar system**—not just on Earth. The one common denominator? **The Sun**.

German professor **Stefan Homburg** shared findings showing that global warming is occurring on multiple planets and moons, suggesting solar fluctuations are the real cause. For example:

- Neptune's moon Triton has warmed by 3 degrees Kelvin.
- Jupiter has experienced a sudden heat wave of 700°C stretching over 130,000 kilometers.
- Saturn is also heating up—though NASA blames its rings, which frankly sounds ridiculous.

- Newly analyzed temperature data show the surface temperature of the moon rose by about three degrees Celsius.

These examples prove that **CO_2 emissions** are not the driving force behind planetary warming. In fact, **CO_2 is vital to life**—it feeds vegetation, plankton, and helps sustain the balance of our atmosphere. Around **95% of greenhouse gases are water vapor**, not CO_2, and minor increases in CO_2 actually enhance plant growth and biodiversity.

Life adapts to warming far more easily than to cooling, yet we're being made to feel guilty for exhaling or driving to work. The real danger lies in the deception being fed to us under the guise of "saving the planet."

Chapter 43

Most Deadliest Executive Order

Now let's turn our attention to something far more immediate—and far more alarming: **Executive Order 14067**, signed by President Biden on **March 9, 2022**. This isn't speculation or hearsay; it's documented, verifiable fact.

The information I'm sharing originates from **Jim Rickards**, a highly respected financial expert and former **advisor to the Pentagon, the White House, and the CIA.** According to Rickards, what happened that day behind closed doors marked one of the most significant turning points in modern American history. With a single signature, President Biden set in motion what many believe to be a **direct assault on financial freedom**—a policy that opens the door to total government control over personal wealth.

Without public consultation, without Congressional debate, and without media transparency, this executive order authorized the development of a **Central Bank Digital Currency (CBDC)**—a programmable digital token that could replace traditional cash. On the surface, it's being marketed as innovation, modernization, and convenience. But beneath that façade lies the potential for **absolute surveillance and manipulation.**

Section 4 of this order is particularly concerning. It establishes the foundation for a financial system in which every transaction can be **tracked, recorded, and controlled.** Imagine a future where your digital wallet can be **frozen, limited, or erased**—not by a hacker, but by government directive. Every purchase, donation, or transfer would become part of a permanent record, accessible to those in power.

Under projects like **Project Lithium** and **Project Hamilton**, these technologies have already been tested for years. They are not theoretical—they are operational. And once implemented nationwide, the shift from cash to digital currency will be irreversible. Paper money will lose its value, and with it, our ability to transact privately or independently.

This so-called "digital dollar" has been described by some experts as **spyware for your wallet**—a financial system designed not for your convenience, but for your compliance. Once cash disappears, every aspect of economic life can be switched on or off with a keystroke.

I cannot emphasize this enough: **we must resist this system before it takes root**. Contact your congressional representatives. Demand public hearings and full transparency about Executive Order 14067 and the future of digital currency in America. This isn't just about economics—it's about the preservation of liberty itself.

Even if this book is copyrighted, I give you **my full permission to copy and share this section freely**. Spread it far and wide. Awareness is our first line of defense, and prayer is our greatest strength. Together, we can still act—before it's too late.

Chapter 44

Timeless Truths for Defeating the Globalists

I now want to share a few essential truths that I discovered through **Brighteon.com**—a platform I strongly recommend for anyone **seeking unfiltered, uncensored information** beyond the limits of mainstream narratives. Over the years, I've come to see that much of what we perceive as "crisis" or "chaos" is not accidental at all—it's engineered.

First, understand this: *scarcity is manufactured*. The food shortages, medicine shortages, and global energy "crises" we hear about daily are not simply the result of natural disaster or bad policy—they are **deliberately orchestrated**. Those who control global supply chains understand that fear is the most effective form of social control. When people are anxious about survival—about whether they can feed their families, heat their homes, or access basic healthcare—they become easier to manipulate.

In truth, **the Earth is abundant**. The planet provides everything necessary for human thriving—sunlight, clean water, fertile soil, and regenerative energy. Yet, through regulatory restrictions, corporate monopolies, and artificial bottlenecks, this abundance is **systematically suppressed**. The illusion of scarcity keeps humanity dependent, docile, and distracted from the truth that **there is enough for all** when resources are shared rather than controlled.

Second, realize this: **our food and health systems are being poisoned**. Pesticides, genetically modified organisms (GMOs), endocrine disruptors, and heavy metals have become normalized components of our diet and environment. These toxins infiltrate our bodies quietly, weakening immune systems, impairing cognitive development, and dulling human vitality. The result is a population that is chemically sedated—fatigued, anxious, and unable to think critically.

No other species on Earth deliberately poisons its young, yet we are told that such contamination is "progress." We're told that lab-grown foods, synthetic chemicals, and "fortified" products are advancements when in truth, they are **tools of biological control**. The slow degradation of human health benefits those who profit from illness and dependency.

And finally, know this: *your mind is powerful beyond measure*. You are not powerless—you are a conduit of **divine creative energy**. Within every human being resides the same force that shapes galaxies, grows forests, and births stars. Your thoughts, your words, and your intentions are frequencies of creation themselves. When directed with clarity and compassion, they ripple outward, transforming the very fabric of reality.

This is the truth that the establishment fears the most: an awakened and united humanity that recognizes its spiritual authority. For when people remember who they are—when they realize they are not subjects of control but architects of creation—the entire machinery of domination begins to crumble.

So remember: while deception may dominate the surface, truth vibrates eternally beneath it. The power has always been within us—**in our awareness, in our unity, and in our unwavering belief that light cannot be extinguished by the shadow.**

Chapter 45

The Deliberate Dumbing Down of America

I've often reflected on the state of education in the United States, and I can't help but see how far we've fallen. The inability of American students to perform on par with most developed nations should alarm everyone, especially given what it means for our country's future and leadership in the world. Twenty-five countries now outperform our K12 students — with China, Hong Kong, Finland, Singapore, South Korea, Japan, and Canada leading the way.

Here at home, our students struggle with even the most basic reading and math skills. A 2024 report revealed that the average score in reading was the lowest since the assessment began in 1992, while math results hit their lowest point since 2005. Over one-third of all 8th graders — and only about 22.8 percent of 12th graders — reach basic proficiency in key subjects like civics, geography, mathematics, reading, science, U.S. history, and writing. That means over 70 percent of our children lack fundamental academic skills after thirteen years of schooling.

The decline isn't sudden. It's part of a slow, deliberate process — one that has allowed ideology and politics to replace true educational outcomes. If you've ever wondered how our school curriculum came to put the population into intellectual slumber, I recommend reading *"The Deliberate Dumbing Down of America"* by Charlotte Iserbyt.

As a whistleblower and former official in the U.S. Department of Education under President Reagan (1981–1982), Iserbyt documented how government bodies, corporations, and foreign groups orchestrated a plan to weaken education. The key was to roll it out gradually so the public wouldn't notice. Her research exposed reform legislation and internal strategies designed to reduce critical thinking and independent learning.

Today, I see the results of that plan everywhere. Our children are not only being dumbed down by the system — we all are. Mobile devices, constant media noise, and filtered information streams have turned people into vessels controlled by what's fed into them through screens.

The internet giants — Google, Wikipedia, and others — act as gatekeepers of information. They manipulate what we see, suppress inconvenient truths, and dictate "official" narratives. In my view, this is no accident. It's part of a coordinated agenda. Add to that the harmful effects of 5G radiation, toxins in our food, and mercury and aluminum in vaccines — and you begin to see a pattern. The dumbing down of humanity is deliberate.

Chapter 46

Admiral Richard Byrd and the Hollow Earth

I've always been fascinated by Admiral Richard Byrd — arguably the greatest polar explorer of the 20th century. In 1925, Byrd set out on a mission to explore some of the most desolate lands on Earth, later earning the highest recognition of achievement for heroism in the country and the greatest military honor.

Byrd was a heroic figure, lauded worldwide as an American pilot, polar explorer, and organizer of polar logistics. Admiral Richard Byrd referred to Antarctica as "The Land of Everlasting Mystery,"

But what makes Byrd especially intriguing is what he may have discovered beneath the ice. According to accounts, including a controversial diary that mysteriously disappeared, Byrd claimed to have found an entry into a hidden world within the Earth — what some call

Agartha. It is often described as a utopian paradise with a capital city called Shamballa, lit by an inner sun, and accessible through secret entrances at the poles.

Agartha is legendary, a subterranean kingdom inhabited by an ancient and technologically advanced civilization. He reported meeting beings incredibly tall, intelligent and very humanoid who welcomed him because of his moral integrity. According to Admiral Byrd, the Agarthians claimed to be the protectors of planet Earth, to protect its inhabitants from the scurrilous activities of the power brokers and nefarious government agencies with impure agendas.

Byrd described traveling over mountains, lakes, rivers, and forests within this inner realm, with temperatures around 74°F. While these claims have been dismissed by mainstream science, they remain compelling. Operation High Jump, a massive 1947 Antarctic expedition that Byrd led, only deepens the mystery. With more than 40 ships, 1,400 men, and heavy military equipment, it was far more than a simple "exploration."

Some researchers believe Operation High Jump aimed to eliminate Nazi bases in Antarctica or seize advanced flying disc technology — theories often tied to rumors that Hitler escaped to Argentina and continued secret operations under the ice.

Later, in 1956, Byrd led another expedition, claiming the North and South Poles were only two of several entrances to the Earth's interior. His close ally, Admiral James Forrestal — the first U.S. Secretary of

Defense — was said to have believed Byrd's accounts. Both men reportedly faced immense pressure to stay silent, and some suggest Forrestal's mysterious death was no accident.

Personally, I own two fascinating books about this subject — Etidorhpa or The End of the Earth by John Uri Lloyd, and The Hollow Earth by Dr. Raymond Bernard. Both reinforce the idea that Byrd wasn't just an explorer, but a truth-teller who dared to reveal what others wanted hidden.

The Mystery of the Moon

I've also pondered deeply on the strange and haunting nature of our moon. Across ancient cultures, it has been revered as **feminine energy**—the quiet counterpart to the sun's fiery force, the motherly guardian of tides and dreams. Yet, beneath that serene glow lies a riddle that modern science still cannot adequately explain. The more I explored, the more I realised that the moon might not be what we've always believed it to be.

During the **Apollo missions**, NASA installed seismic sensors on the lunar surface to measure geological activity. When they intentionally **crashed-landed lunar modules and rockets,** the data stunned scientists—the moon literally **rang like a bell**, resonating for hours. That kind of sustained vibration should be impossible unless the internal structure of the moon was **unlike any natural celestial body** we know. The phenomenon was so striking that even NASA scientists admitted they had no clear explanation.

Some researchers have proposed that the moon might be **partially hollow**, or perhaps composed of materials of **unusual density**. Others, more daringly, suggest that it could be **an artificial construct**—a vast, ancient satellite placed deliberately in Earth's orbit. After all, its size and distance create the perfect conditions for total solar eclipses, an almost miraculous coincidence in cosmic terms. Could such precision really be random?

NASA's explanations for many lunar anomalies have often been **vague or contradictory**, leaving more questions than answers. The patterns of light and shadow on the surface, the strange reflective qualities of certain regions, and the abundance of metals like titanium—all these details seem to hint at something beyond natural formation.

Then there's the work of **Richard C. Hoagland**, who has spent decades analyzing NASA's own imagery and data. His research points toward **geometric structures and patterns**—what he calls "architectural relics"—scattered across the lunar surface, particularly near regions like the far side and the Sea of Tranquility. If true, this suggests that the moon could once have been a station, base, or observatory of some kind—evidence of an intelligence far older than ours.

From my perspective, it's increasingly clear that the **official narrative** surrounding the moon—and indeed much of our **cosmic history**—is incomplete. Whether this omission is due to ignorance, secrecy, or deliberate concealment, I cannot say for sure. But I do know this: the moon watches over us silently, as it has for millennia, holding within its pale surface **the secrets of our origins and the shadows of truths not yet told**.

Chapter 47

Ruby Ridge: An American Tragedy

I often think about Ruby Ridge — an event that so few people today seem to remember, yet one that revealed just how dark and corrupt our government can be. In August 1992, an 11-day siege unfolded in northern Idaho between the federal government and Randy Weaver's family. What started as a dispute over federal firearms charges ended in tragedy — with the deaths of Weaver's wife, Vicki; his 14-year-old son, Sammy; and a U.S. Marshal (Walter 2019).

Randy Weaver had been a U.S. Army engineer before moving his family to a remote cabin on Ruby Ridge. He and his wife, Vicki, wanted to escape what they saw as a decaying, immoral world. They lived as Christian survivalists, believing that a global collapse was imminent. Though they briefly associated with the white supremacist group Aryan Nations, Weaver denied being an active member (Neiwert 2012).

Everything began to spiral in 1989, when Weaver sold two illegal sawed-off shotguns to an undercover ATF informant. When Weaver refused to become an informant himself, the government charged him with weapons violations. Due to a clerical error, he missed his court date and was labeled a fugitive. That's when the government decided to make an example of him.

The siege started on August 21, 1992. A U.S. Marshals surveillance team was spotted by the Weavers' dog. When a marshal shot the dog, young Sammy reacted — and in the exchange that followed, both Sammy and a U.S. Marshal were killed. The following day, an FBI sniper named Lon Horiuchi shot Randy Weaver and then fired again, killing Vicki Weaver as she held her baby in her arms (Walter 2019).

After days of negotiations led by civilian activist Bo Gritz, the standoff finally ended. At the trial that followed, famed lawyer Gerry Spence represented Randy Weaver — and remarkably, Weaver was acquitted of all major charges. Kevin Harris, Weaver's friend, was also acquitted (Neiwert 2012).

Later, the Weaver family received a $3.1 million settlement, and Kevin Harris received $380,000. Investigations that followed sharply criticized the government's actions. The FBI's "shoot on sight" orders were declared unconstitutional, and one agent, E. Michael Kahoe, was convicted for destroying evidence.

To me, Ruby Ridge stands as a warning — a clear message that when citizens are viewed as enemies, tyranny is close behind. It became a rallying cry for many Americans who saw what happened not as justice, but as murder sanctioned by the state. Even Timothy McVeigh later cited Ruby Ridge and the Waco siege as his motivations for the 1995 Oklahoma City bombing — a terrible act that itself came from a place of deep mistrust toward the government (Neiwert 2012).

And Ruby Ridge wasn't the only moment where our own government turned its weapons on civilians.

The Kent State Massacre

On May 4, 1970, another tragedy unfolded on American soil — this time at Kent State University in Ohio. What began as a peaceful student protest against the Vietnam War and the U.S. invasion of Cambodia ended in bloodshed and disbelief. The Ohio National Guard, deployed to control the demonstrations, opened fire on unarmed students, killing four and wounding nine others (Stone, 2000).

These were not violent agitators or armed rebels. They were young men and women — students filled with ideals, courage, and conviction — exercising their First Amendment rights to speak, to assemble, and to stand against what they believed was an unjust war. Despite official orders banning rallies, hundreds gathered on the campus commons to express their outrage over America's deepening military entanglements in Southeast Asia.

Then came the sound that shattered the nation's conscience: a sudden volley of live gunfire that lasted only 13 seconds but changed history forever. When the smoke cleared, Jeffrey Miller, Allison Krause, Sandra Scheuer, and William Schroeder lay dead. Their names would become etched into the collective memory of a generation — symbols of innocence lost, of democracy wounded by its own defenders (Stone, 2000).

The Kent State massacre sent shockwaves across the country. It ignited an unprecedented wave of protests — more than four million students walked out of classrooms, and hundreds of campuses shut down in solidarity. It wasn't just about Vietnam anymore; it was about trust, freedom, and the terrifying realization that the government could turn its guns on its own people. The iconic photograph of a young woman kneeling over Jeffrey Miller's lifeless body became a haunting emblem of national grief and outrage.

In the aftermath, commissions were formed, apologies issued, and blame deflected, but the wound remained. For many Americans, Kent State marked the moment when the veil of patriotic certainty was torn away. It exposed the fragile boundary between liberty and control, between civil dissent and state violence.

Whenever I think about Kent State, one question lingers in my mind: if the First Amendment guarantees our right to protest, assemble, and speak freely, why did the government answer peaceful dissent with bullets? And more importantly, have we really learned from it, or are we still repeating the same mistakes under new names and justifications?

Chapter 48

Mysterious Happenings on the Planet Mars

Now, let me turn to something that few dare to discuss — what's really happening beyond our planet. I've been privileged to hear lectures from several whistleblowers with inside knowledge of classified programs, and what they've revealed is astonishing.

Senator Daniel K. Inouye once said, *"There exists a shadowy government with its own Air Force, its own Navy, its own fundraising mechanism, and the ability to pursue its own ideas of national interest, free from all checks and balances, and free from the law itself."* That statement alone should make you think.

According to multiple insiders, humans have been traveling to Mars for decades (Goode 2016). One of them, Corey Goode who is *a writer, producer, director, and Co-Founder of Disclosure Media* – Books. He was also a former participant in what he calls the "Secret Space Program" — claims that the U.S. established a fleet called Solar Warden in the 1980s, responsible for interplanetary travel and colonization (Goode 2016).

He insists that under Project Solar Warden, underground bases were built on Mars and other celestial bodies. Another whistleblower, known only as Captain Kaye, said he served as a Marine protecting five human colonies on Mars from indigenous life forms. He even claimed to have spent years aboard a massive space carrier before returning to Earth (Kaye 2014).

I know how wild this sounds — but when you hear the same story from multiple independent sources, it's hard to dismiss entirely. The very fact that the "Powers That Be" have well-established secrets and high levels of alien technology that they do not want to be made public.

Adding to this, former CIA pilot John Lear — son of the inventor of the Lear Jet — stated that the Mercury and Apollo missions were diversions to distract the public from real secret operations (Lear 1993). According to him, humans landed on Mars as early as 1966 and have been building colonies there ever since. He even said that NASA has recovered alien technology from crashes dating back to the 1950s.

Then there's the infamous "Face on Mars" — that haunting 1976 image captured by NASA's Viking 1 orbiter, showing what looks uncannily like a human face in the Cydonia region. NASA insists it's just shadows, but I've looked at those images myself, and honestly — you be the judge.

To me, it's obvious that much of what we're told about space is carefully filtered. Technology and discoveries that could change humanity are buried under layers of secrecy. The question is: Why?

183

Chapter 49

The Transhumanist Agenda and Its Focus on Food

I remember the first time I came across this story — it didn't take long before the alternative media world lit up with it. I was honestly stunned when I heard attorney Thomas Renz talking about how the U.S. government had been quietly working on integrating vaccines into our food for nearly twenty years. That's right — the very food on our tables.

When Renz sat down with Naomi Wolf, Ph.D., on April 2, 2025, his words hit me like a ton of bricks. He said, *"Bill Gates, the WHO, and a ton of universities were all talking about including mRNA vaccinations as part of the food. They're going to modify the genes of these foods to make them mRNA vaccines."* Hearing that, I thought — of course they don't want us to know what they're doing.

What really shook me was learning about the enormous pushback from Big Ag lobbyists when a bill came up that would have required transparency on this issue. It made sense though — if people found out that foods might be vaccinated with mRNA or genetically modified to deliver vaccines, the entire agricultural and pharmaceutical web could start to crumble.

Renz suggested something I've since come to believe myself: that the transhumanist agenda — the idea of merging humans with technology and altering us on a genetic level — is being advanced in ways most people can't imagine. Using food as a delivery system for gene therapy sounds like science fiction, but I've seen enough to know how quietly these programs unfold.

I often ask myself, do they not understand what these genetic therapies in livestock could do to us, or do they understand it perfectly — and that's exactly why they're hiding it?

It's no secret that globalists like Klaus Schwab, the founder of the World Economic Forum, have openly admitted their plans to change humanity — not just socially, but genetically. The combination of artificial intelligence, nanotechnology, and gene manipulation is no longer theoretical. And COVID-19, in my view, was their test run — a massive global experiment under the guise of "public safety."

At the end of the day, I can't shake the belief that if enough of us become aware of what's going on — if we refuse to stay divided — we can stop this. It goes against everything human rights stand for. It violates the Nuremberg Code. But I still have hope, because truth has a way of surviving even the most powerful deception.

Chapter 50

The Philadelphia Experiment

The story of the Philadelphia Experiment has fascinated me for years, but it wasn't until I started digging deeper that I realized how far the government went to bury it. Sometimes I still get chills thinking about what I've learned.

It all started with the U.S. Navy's attempt to make the destroyer USS Eldridge invisible to enemy radar. They called it Project Rainbow — but we know it as the Philadelphia Experiment. Using the theories of Nikola Tesla and Albert Einstein, they wrapped the ship in miles of heavy cable and ran a current through it to manipulate electromagnetic fields. The goal was to bend light and radar waves — to literally make the ship disappear from radar.

Tesla and Einstein were reportedly both present at the Philadelphia Naval Shipyard. But before the experiment, Tesla left. He apparently warned that the government wasn't considering the safety of the men aboard. Robert Oppenheimer — yes, the same Oppenheimer behind the atomic bomb — was in the control room that day.

When they threw the switch in 1943, something unimaginable happened. The ship was surrounded by a strange green fog — then it vanished. Moments later, the *USS Eldridge* was spotted in Norfolk,

Virginia — hundreds of miles away — before reappearing back in Philadelphia.

They called it a success, but what followed was horrifying. Many of the crew went insane. Some were found embedded in the steel of the ship itself — fused with the hull. Others became intangible or disappeared completely.

Two of those men, Al Bielek and his half-brother Duncan Cameron, later claimed they jumped overboard during the experiment and somehow landed in 1983 at Camp Hero — forty years into the future. There, they said, they met none other than Oppenheimer, who briefed them on everything that had happened and told them they had to return to destroy the equipment trapping the ship in hyperspace.

It sounds unbelievable — I know. But here's the thing: I actually met Al Bielek twice. He came to Denver, Colorado, over a six-year span to give lectures about his experiences. Sitting in that room listening to him speak, I felt like the ground beneath my understanding of reality shifted.

He told us things that would make any rational person's hair stand on end — but looking into his eyes, I believed he had lived through something extraordinary.

I even own a paperback copy of The Philadelphia Experiment: Project Invisibility by William L. Moore and Charles Berlitz. Every time I reread it, I'm reminded that what's dismissed as "conspiracy theory" today often turns out to be hidden truth tomorrow. Here is a picture of the USS Eldridge.

Chapter 51

Skinwalker Ranch

I've always been fascinated by the mysteries surrounding Skinwalker Ranch, located in west Uintah County, Utah, right next to the Uintah and Ouray Indian Reservation. It's often called the UFO ranch, and for good reason — it has more than a 50-year history of strange and unexplainable events. For as long as I can remember, I've read and heard stories about this place being one of the most active sites of paranormal phenomena in the state. There are countless reports of crop circles, poltergeists, glowing orbs, UFOs, and even otherworldly creatures.

When I first learned about the family that owned the ranch from 1994 to 1996, I was stunned by their experiences. They claimed there were nearly a hundred incidents — cattle disappearing or mutilated, strange lights in the sky, invisible forces that emitted strong magnetic fields, and even large creatures with glowing red eyes that bullets couldn't harm. I couldn't imagine what it must have been like living through that.

Then came Robert T. Bigelow, a businessman who believed that understanding such phenomena was vital to the survival of humanity. He formed the National Institute for Discovery Science (NIDS) and bought the ranch in 1996 to study it. What they uncovered only deepened the mystery. Researchers reported stargates and strange magnetic fields, and even more unexplainable events that couldn't be dismissed as simple myths.

The surrounding area had long been associated with cattle mutilations, and when Bigelow bought the property for $200,000, it was largely because he had heard so many convincing stories from Terry Sherman, the previous owner. Years later, I came across *Hunt for the Skinwalker* by Colm Kelleher and George Knapp. They described the NIDS investigation in vivid detail — UFO sightings, poltergeists, glowing orbs, and strange creatures unlike anything known to science.

What really caught my attention was when James Lacatski from the Defense Intelligence Agency read the book, visited the ranch, and experienced something supernatural himself. That led him to contact Harry Reid and Ted Stevens, who helped secure $22 million from the Department of Defense to study unidentified aerial phenomena. To me, that said a lot — this wasn't just folklore; even the government took it seriously.

Chapter 52

Important Lessons from Ancient History

There's a quote I often think about from Winston Churchill: "Those who fail to learn from history are doomed to repeat it." And I've come to believe that deeply. Over the years, I've studied parts of ancient history that most people have never even heard of — stories that reveal cycles of destruction and rebirth that seem to echo through time.

One such story is about a planet called Maldek, said to have once existed between Mars and Jupiter. It was a lush, green world, advanced and abundant, where robots handled menial tasks and people lived in comfort. Yet, comfort bred complacency. The people of Maldek, much like us today, became self-indulgent and power-hungry. The inhabitants had discovered a rudimentary form of space travel, and could control their weather so that drought and famine became long forgotten.

Then came a mental plaque. It probably started subtly in the minds of those few men of science who shunned the procrastinating majority, in a fervent search for material conquest, thus leaving themselves open to this incurable affliction. The mental disease manifested itself as a lust for greater power.

Eventually, they found the means to create the hydrogen bomb ---- and in a single act of destruction, they obliterated their own planet and murdered the whole populace in one blinding flash of searing flame. All that is now left of that beautiful planet is the **asteroid belt**.

What struck me most about this story is the karmic justice that followed. According to ancient teachings, the souls of Maldek's people had to reincarnate on Earth under strict limitations — our planet accepted them out of compassion, even though it meant enduring their flaws once again.

And sadly, this wasn't the only time. There were also the civilizations of **Lemuria and Atlantis** — both highly advanced, both destroyed by the same lust for power and the misuse of atomic energy.

Lemuria flourished once, forming connections with beings from other worlds. But when greed and division set in, they too unleashed forces beyond control, splitting their continent and destroying themselves. Atlantis followed the same pattern — greatness shadowed by arrogance, wisdom drowned by the pursuit of domination.

Every time I read about these civilizations, I see parallels to our world today. We've once again harnessed the atom, divided ourselves, and allowed technology to outpace wisdom. But unlike before, I believe the outcome can be different. Earth's frequencies are rising, and her ascension to a higher dimension is near. Maybe this time, we'll finally learn.

Chapter 53

The Myth of Pearl Harbor

When I was growing up, I was taught the same story about Pearl Harbor as everyone else — that it was a surprise attack on December 7, 1941, that crippled the U.S. Pacific Fleet and forced America into World War II. But the more I researched, the more I realized that much of that story doesn't hold up. In fact, it's more myth than truth.

I discovered that as early as January 27, 1941, Joseph C. Grew, the U.S. ambassador to Japan, had already warned Washington about Japan's plans for an attack on Pearl Harbor. Later, U.S. intelligence even intercepted messages from Japan's navy asking for detailed maps of ship positions in the harbor — yet, this information was never shared with the commanders stationed there.

By the time Japan's strike force left for Hawaii in late November 1941, the U.S. had intercepted over a thousand messages, many of them clearly pointing to Pearl Harbor as the target. Astonishingly, these were all withheld from the base officers.

Even on the night before the attack, US intelligence decoded a message pointing to Sunday morning as a deadline for some kind of Japanese action. The message was delivered to the Washington high command more than four hours before the attack on Pearl Harbor. But, as many messages before, it was withheld from the Pearl Harbor commanders.

And here's where it gets even more suspicious — the ships destroyed that day were mostly old and slow. The aircraft carriers, which were the real backbone of the Pacific Fleet, had conveniently been sent away days before. To me, that didn't sound like a coincidence. It sounded like a strategy. Roosevelt, it seems, wanted a reason to enter the war — and provoking Japan provided that.

Lieutenant Commander Arthur McCollum even drafted an eight-step plan to push Japan into attacking. Roosevelt followed it almost exactly, and by the time the attack came, everything had been set in motion. Looking back, I can't help but agree with George Graham Vest's words from 1891: *"History is written by the victors and framed according to the prejudices and bias existing on their side."* Maybe that's why we never hear the full story.

Chapter 54

Crop Circles

Crop circles have always fascinated me — those intricate, otherworldly patterns that appear overnight in fields across the globe. They've been showing up for over half a century now, and despite what skeptics say, I can't shake the feeling that there's more to them than simple hoaxes.

Sure, I remember hearing about Doug Bower and Dave Chorley, the two Englishmen from the 1970s who claimed they made a hundred crop circles using ropes and boards. Maybe they did, but there is no way they could create extremely complex crop circles. I've seen the photos, the geometric perfection, the magnetic anomalies found in the soil — things that just don't add up.

Every year, farmers wake up to find massive, complex formations spanning acres of land — in England, yes, but also in Australia, the Netherlands, the U.S., France, and beyond. These patterns seem intentional, almost like messages. Some believe they're from extraterrestrial sources, others say they're interdimensional energy imprints.

I've read theories from scientists who say it could be natural forces — plasma vortices, earth energies, or electromagnetic phenomena. I ask you, who are they trying to fool? And after seeing documentaries like

Crop Circle Realities and reading books like *Secrets in the Fields,* I can't help but feel that something far greater is at play here.

Whatever their true origin, I know this — crop circles challenge us to look beyond what we can easily explain. They remind us that not everything on this planet is as simple or as random as we think.

Here are some amazing pictures of crop circles.

Chapter 55

Stranger at the Pentagon

Valiant Thor is an immortal who resides inside the planet Venus. Yes, the planet Venus is also hollow, along with the planet Mars. He is the commander of Victor One, a spaceship that was stationed on the ground near Lake Mead, Nevada, and he heads the Council of Twelve on Venus.

In March of 1957, Valiant Thor landed in a small craft in Alexandria, Virginia, a city on the Potomac River, a stone's throw from Washington, D.C., and subsequently met with President Dwight D. Eisenhower, Vice President Richard Nixon, and the Chiefs of Staff. The Commander was offered a three-year furnished apartment at the Pentagon.

In December 1959, Dr. Frank E. Stranges met Commander Valiant Thor, and they enjoyed a fine friendship until Dr. Stranges' passing in November 2008. Dr. Frank E. Stranges was a Christian evangelical minister, ufologist, author, and founder of the National Investigations Committee on Unidentified Flying Objects.

The purpose of Valiant Thor's visit was to help the Earth's family lead lives based on spiritual principles, which ensure wholesome progress in all fields of endeavor, including health, economics, scientific and advanced technical knowledge, justice, education, and governance. He also came to promote peace and to warn against the dangers of nuclear weapons, poverty, and environmental destruction. Although his aid was refused by the American government, to this day, Valiant Thor and his companions continue to assist the people of Earth. You need to ask yourself: why did the American government refuse his aid?

Official documentation and signed witness statements, including some from people described as "high-ranking government officials," exist confirming his visitation. The most commonly told version of the story was that Thor lived in the basement of the Pentagon for three years and had regular meetings with President Eisenhower, Vice President Richard Nixon, and senior members of the armed forces. He's also alleged to have met with a number of scientists and religious leaders, appeared at the United Nations headquarters in New York City, and even attended a church in Alexandria, where he preached messages of love and peace.

Valiant Thor's legend endures as a symbol of hope and cosmic benevolence, and indeed, many of these supposed messages are meant to help people come together for the common good—transitioning to clean energy sources, promoting peace over hate, and encouraging environmental awareness. The narrative also aligns with broader themes of extraterrestrial intelligence seeking to guide humanity toward a more enlightened and harmonious future.

Details of this encounter can be found in Dr. Frank E. Stranges' book *"Stranger at the Pentagon."* A short film entitled *Stranger at the Pentagon* was also created. From the above information, you should be able to clearly see that our U.S. government does not want us to live in peace and to have all the advanced technologies that Thor had to offer.

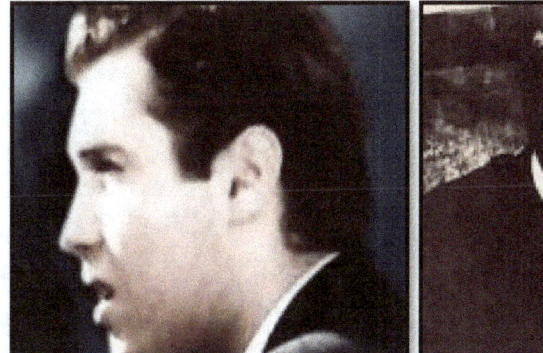

Here are two pictures of Valiant Thor.

I'm going to leave you with a fun fact that will greatly interest fans of The Beatles. I have been a huge Beatles fan for most of my life.

Chapter 56

Former Ringo Starr Startling Information

"REAL" PAUL MCCARTNEY DIED IN 1966 AND WAS REPLACED BY A LOOK-ALIKE

The former drummer of the Beatles, Ringo Starr, surprised the world during an interview in his luxurious Californian residence when he admitted that the 45-year-old rumors about the alleged death of Paul McCartney in 1966 were actually true.

In an exclusive interview with the *Hollywood Inquirer*, Mr. Starr explained that the "real" Paul McCartney had died in a car crash on November 9, 1966, after an argument during a Beatles recording session. To spare the public from grief, the Beatles replaced him with a man named William Shears Campbell, who was the winner of a McCartney look-alike contest and who happened to have the same kind of jovial personality as Paul. Here is what Ringo said:

"When Paul died, we all panicked!" claims Ringo, obviously very emotional. "We didn't know what to do, and Brian Epstein, our manager, suggested that we hire Billy Shears as a temporary solution. It was supposed to last only a week or two, but time went by and nobody seemed to notice, so we kept playing along. Billy turned out to be a pretty good musician, and he was able to perform almost better than Paul. The only problem was that he couldn't get along with John at all."

He notably says that the entire *Sgt. Pepper's Lonely Hearts Club Band* album was awash with *"Paul is dead"* clues: the Beatles had indeed officially formed a "new" band featuring a "fictional" member named Billy Shears, which happened to be the actual name of Paul's replacement.

"We felt guilty about the deception," added Ringo Starr. *"We wanted to tell the world the truth, but we were afraid of the reactions it would provoke. We thought the whole planet was going to hate us for all the lies we had told, so we kept lying but sending subtle clues to relieve our consciousness. When the first rumors finally began about the whole thing, we felt very nervous and started fighting a lot with each other. At some point, it was too much for John, and he decided to leave the band."*

Ringo Starr claims that he finally decided to tell the truth because he was afraid that it was going to die with him. At age 74, he is the only other surviving member of the famous band besides the fake Paul McCartney, and he feared the deception would never be revealed. Mr. Starr alleges that the group did send out many hidden messages through the years to prepare the population for the truth.

Below are the pictures of the real Paul McCartney on the left and the fake Paul on the right. You can clearly see the difference in the structure of their faces.

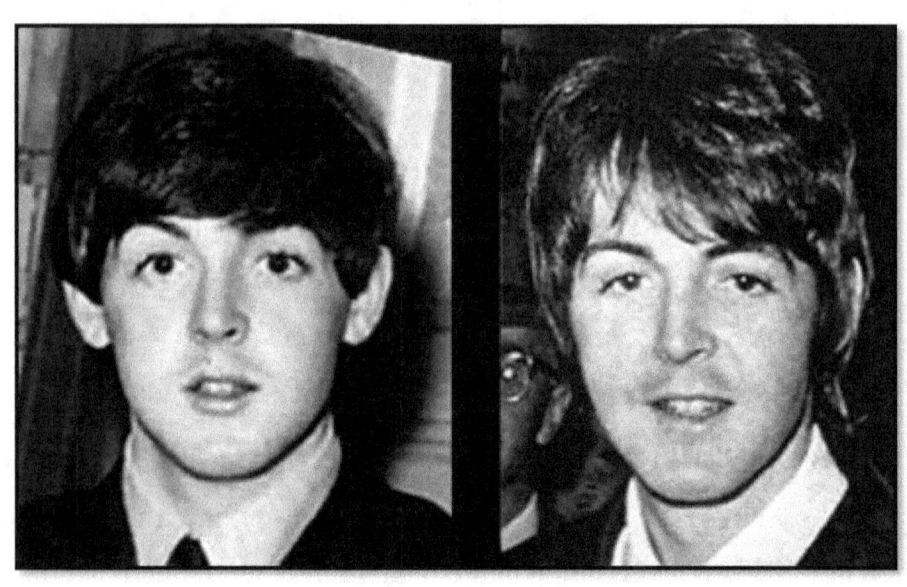

Chapter 57

Brief Summary

My Commentary on Political Corruption

The following is a commentary that I wrote in response to a question someone had posed: "How do you clean up corruption in our politics?"

The answer to this question is quite simple. We need to have laws that completely eliminate all lobbyists and reduce the term limits for all members of Congress to eight years, just like the term limits for our presidents. It's true that the longer a person is in Congress, the more power they wield. It's a common axiom that power corrupts.

Also, the amount of money that a corporation contributes to a candidate for re-election should have a strict set limit. The more money a corporation gives to a candidate, the more influence it has over that candidate. Unfortunately, I do not see any of these concepts being activated or initiated.

I also want to leave you with some important quotes from one of our most intelligent U.S. Presidents, Thomas Jefferson, the father of our Constitution:

"A private central bank issuing the public currency is a greater menace to the liberties of the people than a standing army. We must not let our rulers load us with perpetual debt."

"I believe that banking institutions are more dangerous to our liberties than standing armies."

"The constitutions of most of our States assert that all power is inherent in the people; that... it is their right and duty to be at all times armed."

"The course of history shows that as government grows, liberty decreases."

"Does the government fear us? Or do we fear the government? When the people fear the government, tyranny has found victory. The federal government is our servant, not our master!"

You need to keep these quotes from President Thomas Jefferson foremost in your mind. There you have it in a nutshell. You need to realize that just by the fact that you have read this report, you now know more than 80% of the people on the planet. As I have already said, things are going to get better over time — but we just have to be patient. Remember the phrase, *"It's always darkest before the dawn."*

The following is a commentary that I wrote answering a question that someone had posed. The question is "How do you clean up corruption in our politics"? The answer to this question is quite simple. We need to have laws that completely eliminate all lobbyists and to reduce the term limits to all members of Congress to 8 years, just like the term limits of our presidents. It's true that the longer a person is in Congress, the more power they wield. It's a common axiom that power corrupts".

Also the amount of money that a corporation contributes to a candidate for reelection should have a strict set limit. The more money a corporation gives to a candidate, the more influence it has over the candidate. Unfortunately, I do not see any of these concepts being activated and initiated. I also want to leave you with some important quotes from one of our most intelligent U.S. Presidents, President Thomas Jefferson, the father of our Constitution.

"A private central bank issuing the public currency is a greater menace to the liberties of the people than a standing army. We must not let our rulers load us with perpetual debt". "I believe that banking institutions are more dangerous to our liberties than standing armies".

"The constitutions of most of our States assert that all power is inherent in the people; that... it is their right and duty to be at all times armed".

"The course of history shows that as government grows, liberty decreases"

"Does the government fear us? Or do we fear the government? When the people fear the government, tyranny has found victory. The federal government is our servant, not our master!" You need to keep these quotes from President Thomas Jefferson foremost in your mind.

There you have it in a nutshell. Just by the fact that you have read this report you know more than 80% of the people on the planet. As I have already said, things are going to get better over time but we just have to be patient. Remember the phrase "It's always darkest before the dawn".

Addendum

Confirmation: The Major cause of Autism

A top expert has issued explosive testimony warning that CDC data shows Covid mRNA shots caused far more harm to public health than any supposed benefit. Dr. Toby Rogers, Ph.D., provided the bombshell testimony during a Senate hearing last month.

As a leading expert, Dr. Toby Rogers, Ph.D., dropped an explosive testimony to warn that data from the U.S. Centers for Disease Control and Prevention (CDC) proves that Covid mRNA "vaccines" did far more harm to public health than any supposed benefit. He provided the bombshell testimony during a Senate hearing in October 2025.

Dr. Rogers explains that the CDC's own research determined that mRNA injections have "negative efficacy." Yet, the CDC and other health officials continued to push the "safe and effective" narrative. Rogers demanded when speaking to Congress, "Tell me how a vaccine with negative efficacy is saving lives."

Dr. Rogers spent nearly a decade researching the rise of autism in our country due to the very fact that his son was autistic. He was desperate to find the answer. He told senators that published evidence shows vaccines and environmental toxins are the most likely culprits behind the epidemic now affecting millions of American children.

"I went to the CDC's webpage on the causes of autism," Rogers explained, "As a Ph.D. student, I was trained to focus on primary source documents, so I read all of the references in their footnotes. "To my surprise, I quickly discovered that the CDC's narrative did not add up."

He also noted the lack of urgency from the federal government, despite autism's cost already reaching "hundreds of billions of dollars."

Why on all Legal Documents, is Your Name in all Caps?

If you were to Google this question, you would find the first few passages stating it's just a formality for clarification, plus it is a convenient way for our government to recognize you. This is pure Bull Shit! Here is the real reason.

Your legal name is the name that the government likes to use to attach your identity (set of fictitious characteristics) to it, allowing the government to identify you. You need to know that your legal name is not the name given to you by your mother and father; instead, it is a name created by the government to make it easier for you to do business with its corporations. However, the government likes to use your legal name as a tool to control you, so it is wise to learn how to use your legal name wisely.

To be more specific, your legal name is the name of a corporation created under your given name. The government uses your legal name to attach you to a dead fictional character. This allows the government to identify you and do business with you. Because of this, if you want to free yourself from its jurisdiction successfully, you need to stop thinking that your legal name is who you are.

The evidence that names are designations of artificial persons or legal fictions can be found in the legal definition of the word name. *Black's Law Dictionary* (6th edition) defines the word name using these exact words: "The designation of an individual person, or of a firm or corporation." The word corporation is defined by the same law dictionary as, "An artificial person or legal entity created by or under the authority of the laws of a state." Based on the definitions in this paragraph, in law, a name is a designation of a corporation which is an artificial person.

The process that allows the government to legally claim you as a corporation involves the creation of an artificial person (fictitious character), which is a legal name often written in all capital letters, and then tricking you into agreeing to be that artificial person or legal name. This legal name was created shortly after you were born and was recorded on a bond. This bond that records the date of your person's birth is known as a birth certificate.

Again, know that you have been conned and deceived by our government.

www.ingramcontent.com/pod-product-compliance
Lightning Source LLC
Chambersburg PA
CBHW071730120626
46550CB00002B/462